COLLECTING OURSELVES

One year of Experiments & Devotionals On Finding the Peace of Christ For Flight, Fight or Freeze

Dionne Carpenter

ISBN 978-1-7349152-0-4
ISBN 13: 978-1-7349152-0-4 (Wild Socks Press)

Published by Wild Socks Press
Requests for information should be directed to Dionne Carpenter at Wild Socks Press
www.wildsockspress.com
dionne@wildsockspress.com

DEDICATED

To the God of Peace
and the Captain of the Hosts of heaven
with gratitude too deep for words,
and to you, Gentle Reader,
as you pursue the peace of Christ.

Now may the Lord of peace Himself
give you peace at all times and in every way….
II Thessalonians 3:16

ALSO BY DIONNE CARPENTER

Trust Training:
A Field Manual for Confident Trust in God
Before, During and After Life's Battles

Trading Voices:
Creating Space for the Healing Voice of Jesus
to End the Torment of Self-Loathing

Winning the Hearts of Those you Lead:
12 Principles for New Pastors from the
Rise to Power of Saul and David

MAJOR CONTRIBUTOR TO

Daily Encouragement in the Church Planting Journey:
365 Days of Wisdom, Inspiration and Courage
for Church Planters by Church Planters

ALSO PUBLISHED BY WILD SOCKS PRESS

Leaning into the Wind
and Other Stories
by Jim Carpenter

ACKNOWLEDGEMENTS

Unlike other book projects, I went into this one with no idea where the year would take me or what I'd learn through the process. So it blessed my heart to have such great friends and allies along the journey, even before we got around to polishing this manuscript.

As always, I'm grateful for the many ladies in my Trust Training Bible study and several wonderful clients who joined with me to do experiments of their own. Their unique stories expanded the opportunity to experiment beyond my own limited situation to find general principles, not just personal lessons. Our insights and reactions, setbacks and victories, gave me plenty of food for thought. You will see times when they spurred significant new avenues of exploration as the year unfolded.

My hard working beta readers love me but aren't afraid at all to challenge me to do my best. Thank you so much to Julie Anderson, Jerleen Bezzo, Jordan Busa, Lisa Butler, Ann Dokken, Kerrie Nelson, Karen Northrup and Pat Thomas who all went above and beyond to make this book more user friendly.

I owe a huge debt of gratitude to Terri Palmer who solved a thorny formatting issue after I beat my head against a wall for weeks.

I owe another huge debt of gratitude to Kat Jones, the gifted photographer of Figure #8 on page 18, and for all the moms and beautiful daughters who braved Covid-19 fears one delightful morning to get their photos taken with my inscrutable stuffed hippo. You're awesome!

Last but definitely not least, my husband Jim is always my first reader and the editor I rely on the most. I especially appreciate his insistence for this book that I keep it grounded in the Scriptures even when exploring purely neurological discoveries. For all of our life together, Jim has modeled the beatitude grace of peacemaking. It's one of the many reasons I wake up every morning grateful to God for one more precious day with the love of my life.

TABLE OF CONTENTS

PART I: HOW OUR AMAZING BRAIN KEEPS US SAFE

1. ONE YEAR OF EXPERIMENTS: INTRODUCTION

2. HOW OUR BRAIN PROCESSES FEAR & TRAUMA

3. ONE YEAR OF EXPERIMENTS: THREE TESTS

PART II: OUR EXPERIMENTS ON FINDING THE BETTER WAY TO BE SAFE

4. SILLY ACTS OF OBEDIENCE

14. FINAL EXAM: STAYING AT PEACE FOR THE HOLIDAYS

15. ONE YEAR OF EXPERIMENTS: RESULTS

APPENDIX

PART I

HOW OUR AMAZING BRAIN KEEPS US SAFE

For You created my inmost being;
You knit me together in my mother's womb.
I praise You because I am fearfully and wonderfully made;
Your works are wonderful, I know that full well.
Psalm 139:13, 14

1
One Year of Experiments: Introduction

Welcome! Welcome to a Fascinating Year!

I'm thrilled that you picked up this book. Everything about this project I propose to do this year covers intriguing recent discoveries in brain science and explores untamed territory in the human heart. On one level, I'm scared to death to tackle my own deepest fears and anxieties in such a public way. Any exploration of Survivor Mode by definition gets us into territory of our most embarrassing insecurities. But on another level, I'm happy to push the envelope and boldly blow the doors off because I have this gut feeling that the rewards will far exceed any temporary discomfort.

A BIT OF MY STORY TO SET THE STAGE FOR THIS BOOK

In one way or another, my entire life has been a quest to overcome fear. I grew up in a pretty dysfunctional family ruled by an angry, unpredictable father who molested me for years, and a crazy-making mother who demanded strict obedience to the family rules, such as "Thou shalt not tell the secret." I spent most of my childhood looking okay to outsiders but privately lurching from trauma to trauma where my fear regularly flipped me into Flight Mode or the dreary depression of Freeze Mode.

Ironically, the worst of it was that my parents were also well respected missionaries, pastors and beloved Bible teachers as part of a great legacy of grandparents, aunts and uncles who had faithfully served the Lord with genuine sincerity. The Christian part of my childhood gave me a sincere love for Jesus and an extensive foundation of Bible knowledge. But the crushing dysfunction broke my ability to trust God.

I served the God of the Bible with all my heart but I was scared to death of Him.

After I left home I married a wonderful man who had been called to ministry. While we planted four churches and served in other great ministries, behind the scenes I struggled to recover and find healing from my childhood traumas.

I had a head full of knowledge about what I should be doing, especially about how to pray. But my attempts at having a satisfying prayer life frustrated and defeated me. Most of all, I longed to trust God fully and that singular ache in my soul drove me year after year to keep at it. I deeply regretted the lost decades while I struggled in vain to break free from brokenness. In fact, I would beg God to someday restore to me "the years that the locusts had eaten," as He promised in Joel 2:25.

About twenty years ago I had a major breakthrough that allowed me to reconnect with God when someone introduced me to listening prayer. At long last, the Lord had opened a channel for me to connect with Him in a meaningful way. I felt like a newborn baby just starting to talk. For two years, I devoted myself to learning to distinguish His voice from all the other random thoughts and voices of self-loathing or enemy accusation in my head.

I asked Him to teach me how to trust Him and He did so. (The *Trust Training* Bible Study discusses this in more detail.) I also asked God to make me a woman of peace. I had only known angst and inner turmoil, even while trying to recover, and I had no idea how to "do peace" or live without fear or anxiety.

For almost twenty years I have had this curious Teacher/Student relationship with God as He restores to me those lost years. (By the way, please bear in mind as you read my story that you are catching me in my sixty-sixth year of a life-long pursuit of God and that for the first 48 I couldn't have written any of it! I am definitely a late bloomer when it comes to enjoying a flourishing prayer life.)

So, anyway, nowadays, each New Year's Day, I take a prayer retreat to pray for the coming year and each year He gives me a clear assignment of what to meditate on and study in more depth. Several of those year-long assignments have tackled longstanding fears and helped build new mindsets to replace residual dysfunction. As you will see, the project for this year comes out of that tradition. I'm confident to bring you along for the ride because God has been such a reliable teacher in the past that I'm not afraid to let you eavesdrop a little on that precious side of my relationship with Him.

OK, switching gears. My personal breakthrough became the springboard for a new calling to become a Trauma Counselor which I have thoroughly enjoyed. After seven years of intensive training, I have loved this new ministry of helping clients recover from their own traumas. I love that the learning never stops and it gets more fun the longer I do it. Just below our superficial differences, we all deal with the same sorts of fears and insecurities. It fills me with joy to put on my "Trail Guide" hat and help other travelers navigate the path to wholeness I know so well.

NEW DISCOVERIES ABOUT THE BRAIN

We've learned more about the brain in the last thirty years than has been known in all the rest of recorded history. Only recently have scientists all over the world developed sophisticated instruments to study actively functioning brains, not just MRI snapshots or dissection of cadaver brains.

And after these scientists began to map the parts of the brain and their functions, it took a while for them to get around to studying what the brain does when faced with fear and danger, and how it recovers afterwards. People had a vague idea but nowhere near what we have learned lately.

So we had these new tools in place at this exact time in history, just when we were suffering back-to-back catastrophes like the 9/11 terrorist strike, the wars in Iraq and Afghanistan and the aftermath of the Katrina hurricane. Many of these unfortunate soldiers were coming home with PTSD (Post Traumatic Stress Disorder). In earlier wars, like the two World Wars and Vietnam, the medical experts fumbled around and mostly let trauma victims heal on their own or with talk therapy and plenty of antidepressants. That is, when they didn't ignore or look down their noses at those who struggled.

One of the few blessings to come from all that recent tragedy has been that since we had many, many newly traumatized people hanging about, scientists focused on studying the brains of these people who had PTSD or had survived a disaster. They made astounding new discoveries, some of which I'm delighted to share in this book. It's intriguing to see how the brain works.

We all have this elegantly designed neurological system to deal with danger called Survivor Mode that flips us into Flight, Fight or Freeze Mode whenever needed. We don't need to dread it or feel ashamed of it.

And it's a huge blessing to learn simple strategies to help ourselves handle trauma – immediately – as it unfolds around us, and to regain equilibrium quickly once the crisis has passed. The two simple drills we will learn to use this year do just that.

The books I studied used lots of anatomical jargon, especially about the many overlapping sets of ways to label parts of the brain: the lobes of the brain, left brain/right brain terminology, areas of functionality, the central nervous system and the limbic system, among others.

To make it simpler, and because you're not here to pass an anatomy test but to get a better practical handle on how to master fear, we'll look at three key parts of the Limbic System because that's the specific system in the brain that controls Fight, Flight or Freeze. But you and I will know that the limbic system includes other components I chose not to mention. And the brain itself does much more beyond merely dealing with Survivor Mode.

Agreed?

BRAIN SCIENCE AND BIBLE TRUTH

The Bible does not claim to be a scientific book. But what the Bible says about the brain, the mind and the body is God's truth and so we measure science by the Bible, not the other way around. In fact, after studying the latest research on the brain, I've concluded that the most inclusive description of the brain comes from I Thessalonians 5:23.

> May God Himself, the God of Peace, sanctify you through and through. May your whole **spirit, soul and body** be kept blameless at the coming of our Lord Jesus Christ. [my emphasis]

For all their expertise, brain scientists completely ignore the spiritual aspect of the human mind. They don't include the soul when mapping the brain because they focus only on the physical. Their biases assume that all will be well once we pull ourselves out of Survivor Mode.

Not necessarily true.

Or that sinful humanity will find it an easy task to overcome bad habits of anger, worry or defeatism.

Not at all true.

On the other hand, when Christians give advice on how to manage or overcome fear or anxiety we tend to ignore or minimize how our bodies themselves – and our brains in particular – march to their own drummer during scary situations. We favor top-down strategies like reading and memorizing more Bible verses, praying to God, and powering through or completely ignoring the powerful, visceral turmoil within our body.

So when a crisis hits, sometimes we can rise up with confident faith and sail above any bodily reaction. But more often than we care to admit, our bodies hijack all our good intentions, we get lost in the weeds of our fears, insecurities and adrenaline-driven overreaction, and feel ashamed and defeated afterwards.

I'd like to build a good bridge connecting the best of these two streams of wisdom.

It will help us enormously to become well equipped for crisis if we learn basic information about how the body responds to danger and threat. But that info alone will not solve the bigger problem of how to deal with the catastrophe itself.

On the other hand, it's wonderful to know Bible verses and to strive to trust God in the middle of disaster. And we can more easily achieve that noble goal if we also learn how to work with our body so it doesn't trip us up when we most need to have all our wits about us.

My project this year honors the wisdom learned from both the latest scientific discoveries about how the brain processes fear as well as sound Bible study that teaches us how to come to peace – not only with head knowledge but also with blessed peace in our emotions and our body.

To that end I came up with a working theory.

My Theory

When we notice that our body and our emotions have jumped into Flight, Fight or Freeze Mode, if we ***first*** spend 2-3 minutes doing whichever drill best pulls us back into Normal Mode, and ***then*** pray, we will find it much easier to fully connect with Jesus and find the peace of Christ.

I got really excited by the newfound neurological information and by this opportunity to do some experiments on the topic. I had a hunch other ladies would enjoy participating in such an intriguing project. So we hosted a weekend workshop where I taught more than 60 ladies about how the brain processes trauma. We all learned how to do the two simple and yet surprisingly effective drills that can bring our brain to peace.

The women had a blast learning the new information and it was fun and goofy practicing the new drills. It connected with them and they could see the value of using the drills when adrenaline kicked in. So a number of us continued to play around with them, trying out the drills in a variety of circumstances and sharing our results.

The Lord's hand was all over this project, especially at its inception. I had wanted to create a bridge incorporating the best parts of the new scientific discoveries and the best parts of the wisdom we cherish as Christ followers. When I took my normal January prayer retreat, the Lord gave me the final piece of the equation that brought the balance I needed for my Year of Experiments. You'll read about that as the January 1st entry in Part II of this book.

GETTING UP TO SPEED

Before we launch into our experiments, we need to get up to speed on the most pertinent new discoveries about how the brain functions and how two little brain drills help us control adrenaline. As you'll see, this isn't a formal textbook. I'll use nicknames, goofy cartoons and simple analogies to make it easy to understand.

I presented most of this material at that workshop I mentioned. But the tips on how to do the drills most effectively will include insights my friends and I discovered during our year of experimentation.

2
How our Brain Processes Fear & Trauma

- New Discoveries about the Brain
- How Survivor Mode Works
- Recognizing when we've Flipped into Flight, Fight or Freeze Mode
- Two Drills to Pull us out of Survivor Mode
- The Window of Tolerance and how to Foster Resiliency

1. How the Brain Develops

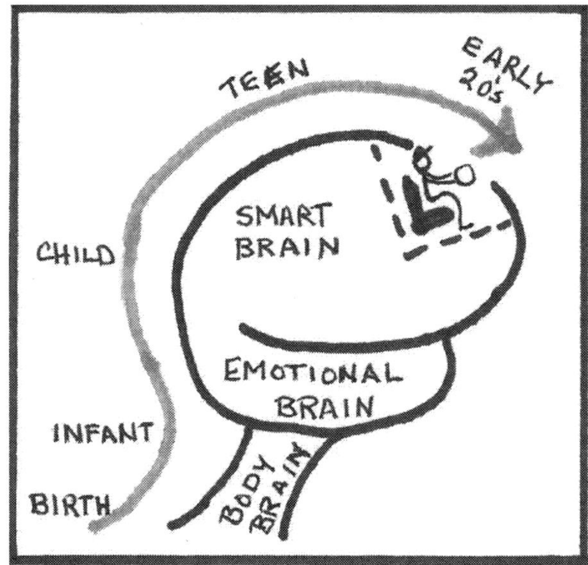

Fig. 1: BRAIN DEVELOPMENT

A healthy newborn baby's head holds an amazing, working brain. However, the baby can't use its entire brain yet because the human brain takes many years to fully develop.

We're talking like 18-24 years or so.

In this overview, we'll focus on Survivor Mode, one of the body functions controlled by the brain. To better understand how it operates, let's first look at how the entire brain develops. In Fig. 2, "Brain Development," the gray curving arrow illustrates that the brain develops from **BOTTOM to TOP.**

AT BIRTH: BODY BRAIN

We have labeled the brain stem "Body Brain" which represents all the **unconscious, automatic** functions like the heart beating, the lungs breathing, the digestive system working, and the gazillion fluids and hormones, etc. getting produced on cue that keep the body functioning. The Body Brain always remains **primitive and totally nonverbal.** Heart, lungs and such MUST function or the baby dies. So the Body Brain must work right from the get go.

INFANT: EMOTIONAL BRAIN

This part of the brain also hits the ground running right from birth and takes 4-5 years to fully develop. But then it always keeps the mindset of a **bright five year old**. Its main job is to build a vast database of info to protect the baby from emotional or physical harm. It learns what to classify as:

- Pleasure or Pain
- Happy or Sad
- "Connected with people" or Abandoned
- Safe or Unsafe

If you startle at a noise, that's Emotional Brain on the case: lightning fast, accessing its database and reacting to protect you from danger. It's also the part that remembers where Mom hid the yummy cookies you crave or why you love roller coasters.

CHILD THROUGH TEEN YEARS: SMART BRAIN

How fully this part of the brain develops depends on the **child's intelligence**, **experiences** in their family and the availability of **schooling**. The first order of business for the developing Smart Brain:

- **Emotionally bonding with parents**,
- **Learning to walk**,
- **Learning to talk**,
- Then expanding **vocabulary and languages**.

As time goes on, the Smart Brain collects **organized memories** the child can recall like trips to the beach, the multiplication tables and **facts and dates**. The child/teen learns **social skills** and a **sense of time**. He/she gains the capacity to know God and memorize Bible verses and develops the **ability to make wise choices** and **reason things out objectively**.

BY THE EARLY 20's: PILOT

The HIGHEST PART of the fully developed brain is the **Pre-frontal Cortex** which we will call the **PILOT** in this book. Like wisdom teeth that don't even show up until the child loses baby teeth, the Pilot comes on board late in the game and develops gradually.

Somewhere around the age of eight to ten years old, a child will become aware of their own mortality and will more intelligently own the responsibility for wrongful actions they have done. In Christian circles this is called the "Age of Accountability." At this point, the child begins to understand the concept of long term consequences and may be able to observe their own behavior. That marks the start of Pilot, like the first wisdom tooth popping out.

The Pilot develops fully when children grow up in emotionally healthy families but development can get stunted in abusive ones.

2. Let Me Introduce you to Pilot

PILOT = Prefrontal Cortex or the **"Observer"** part of the Brain.

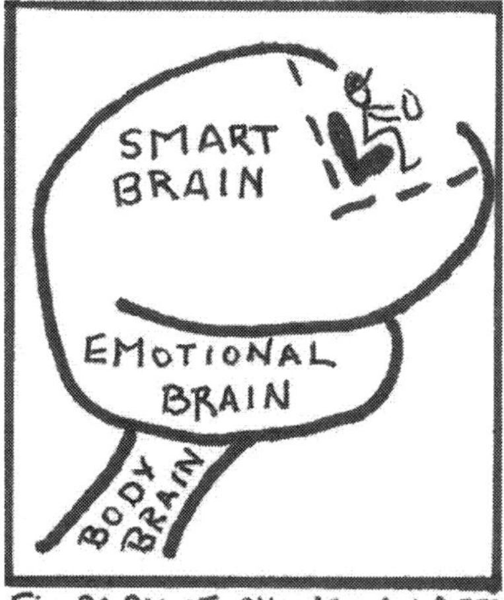

Fig.2: PILOT SHOWS UP LAST

It handles the highest, wisest and most long-range level of thinking. It can think through the likely consequences of potential behavior. As Outside Observer, it can identify what its own brain is feeling, thinking or doing at any given time. See Fig. 3, "Pilot Shows Up Last."

"Hmm. I notice that my thoughts are racing."

"Hmm. I notice that my mind is feeling especially sad today."

We nickname it the Pilot because it steers the ship when the Brain is fully "Collected." It also knows what all the cockpit gauges and instruments mean and how to use that information to get plane safely from one place to another. Let's zero in on how it does this.

Fig. 4, "The Upset Me," illustrates a person gripped by an upsetting emotion or a tormenting thought, or someone caught up in the crisis of the day. Freeze framed in this moment, "Upset Me" really, really believes:

- I = My feeling
- I have no self-awareness beyond this feeling
- This feeling will **always** be my reality

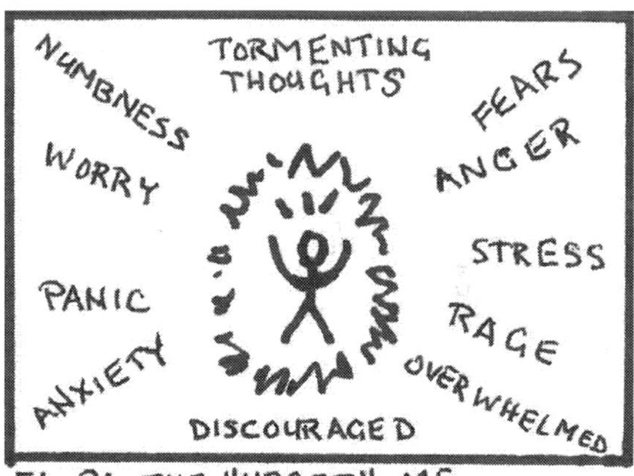

Fig.3: THE "UPSET" ME

Who might think that way?

- A 2 year old having a temper tantrum
- A teenager in the grip of depression
- A panicked adult
- An adult consumed by road rage
- Anyone who has fully flipped into Survivor Mode

However, Fig. 5, "Pilot Steps Back," shows that if we activate our **Pilot**, we can **mentally step back up into an "Observer" stance** and notice the part of our brain in the grip of all those feelings. The "Pilot Me" works most effectively to pull the "Upset Me" out of that upset state if it stays:

- **Calm** and matter-of-fact, not daunted by the freak out
- **Assessing**, like a nurse or a good mom with a sick child
- **Curious** and open to listening
- **Kind** instead of harsh or critical

Fig. 4: PILOT STEPS BACK

We find a great example of Pilot in action in Psalm 42:5. Notice the calm curiosity and the kind encouragement to pull out of discouragement by taking a larger view of the upsetting situation: "Why, my soul, are you downcast? Why so disturbed within me? Put your hope in God, for I will yet praise Him, my Savior and my God."

When Christians step back up into Pilot, we can sense the presence of Jesus with us in that Observer place. In fact, my working theory for the year will test this out in more detail.

3. Time Out: Let's Find and Activate Pilot

Fig. 5: FINDING PILOT

This activity will help us connect with all the players in Fig. 6, "Finding Pilot."

PILOT

Touch your **forehead** (because it's where your prefrontal cortex is). Notice the part of yourself that – in whatever way makes sense to you – would be your Pilot. Use your Pilot to simply **notice** the rest. You might say a quick prayer as you begin: **"Jesus, help me to quiet myself and find You."** Be calm, assessing, curious and kind.

BODY BRAIN

Focus your attention on your breathing. Think to yourself: **"I notice that my breathing right now is ________."** (It could be fast or slow, shallow or deep, comfortable or hyperventilating; doesn't matter.) Then deliberately slow down your breathing just a little.

EMOTIONAL BRAIN

Check around and notice one of your current emotions – doesn't matter which one – and think to yourself: **"I notice that my body is feeling the emotion of ___________ now."**

SMART BRAIN

Check around and notice a thought running through your mind right now. **"I notice that my brain is thinking the thought that________."**

JESUS

Now just relax. Consider that swirl of breathing, feelings and thoughts as if it were outside of you. Open your senses by faith to feel around for the Presence of Jesus. He is here right now with you as the God of Peace. Picture the two of you calmly observing your mind and body.

- Thank Him for your wordless Body Brain that keeps your heart, lungs and every crucial bodily system working night and day.
- Thank Him for your Emotional Brain, always on the case to keep you safe.
- Thank Him for your Smart Brain that has learned so much over the years.
- Thank Him for giving you a Pilot with its potential to bless and enrich your life.
- Then be quiet and leave space for Jesus to speak within your mind or just be with you in companionable silence and peace.

4. Survivor Mode Stars: Amy & Hippo

The Limbic System in the brain handles Survivor Mode. It has multiple working parts within the brain but the most important for our purposes are the three listed in Fig. 7, "The Limbic System:"

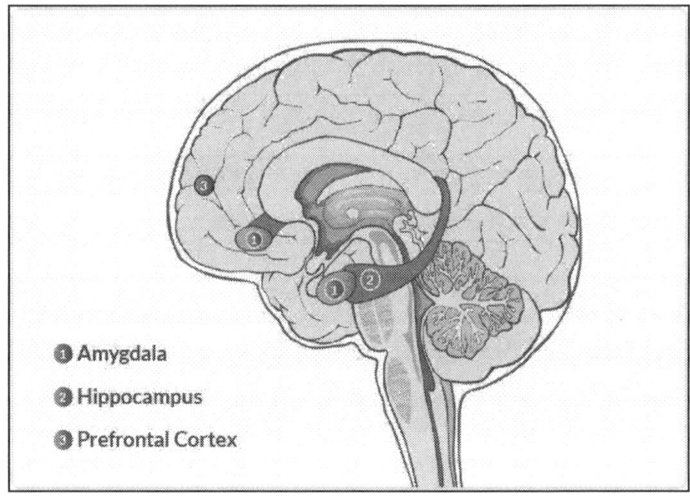

- The Amygdala
- The Hippocampus
- The Prefrontal Cortex

As we've already mentioned, the Prefrontal Cortex doesn't come on line until late in the game as the crowning achievement of the Smart Brain.

Now let's zero in on Survivor Mode, which mainly operates from within the Emotional Brain. Remember we said the Emotional Brain develops from birth to completeness around four or five years of age and stays that mental age for the rest of our lives. This adorable picture, Fig. 8, captures this youthful mental age and gives us an easy way to visualize the lifelong partnership of two out of our three main players in the Emotional Brain.

AMYGDALA: "AMY"

Amygdala is a big and unfamiliar word so we'll dub her "Amy" for short. Amy feels emotions and senses things in the world around her. She's always scanning for danger and sounds the alarm if she senses a physical threat or an emotional threat, like the possibility of getting rejected, disrespected or abandoned.

HIPPOCAMPUS: "HIPPO"

The hippocampus assigns a meaning to the things Amy has spotted. Hippo seems hardwired to know the meaning of some things. For instance, babies don't have to be taught to tense up when a stranger looms over them and invades their space. Every living thing recognizes the mortal danger of a predator swooping down to attack from above and flinches at anything that kinda sorta resembles that primal threat.

But many noises and situations require an explanation. Amy and Hippo work together to sort those things out. The child's personal experience plus the people nearby determine the meaning for each child.

As an example, what does the sound of a siren mean? When I babysat my two year old granddaughter, she alerted at the sound of a siren when a fire engine a few blocks away began to rumble down our street.

She tensed up and asked, "What's that sound?"

I responded happily, "That's a fire truck! Let's run upstairs and watch it pass." I told her that the firemen race to go help someone in trouble. Their truck roars by our window and it sounds scary but it's exciting, not dangerous. Her Hippo files that away under "safe" noises.

But what if the same siren blares in tornado country? This toddler sees the adults all tense up and race for safety down into a scary dark place. The wind and rain rages outside, and the ominous tornado weather sets people on edge. For that child, a "siren" means massive personal "DANGER!"

Same noise interpreted two different ways. The same sound – daddy's footsteps – signals pleasure if he's a fun, loving dad or dread if he's an angry drunk. "Snake" means scary danger in most families but not in the family of snake charmers.

PREFRONTAL CORTEX: PILOT

Many childhood fears naturally lose their terror just by us growing up. I remember when one of my granddaughters was a toddler and she developed a great fear of the purple octopus in one of her early reader books. Amy and Hippo colored that fear in big letters for several years. But it had disappeared on its own by the time she started kindergarten without any help from her Pilot which wouldn't show up for years.

Some childish fears stick with us well into adulthood in the form of emotional insecurities or phobias. They can get deeply entrenched into our fear responses. Unless those get challenged or healed in some way, they won't ever lose their potency.

For those fears, Pilot needs to get involved to help Amy and Hippo modify their early conclusions. The Stand-Down Drill and the Grounding Drill, that we'll discuss more fully starting in Chapter 12, serve us well to deliberately unify all three of our key Limbic System players.

5. The Triune Brain

…a brain with a brain within a brain…. P.D. MacLean

So I'm reading along in these books describing the latest discoveries about the brain and an almost palpable awkwardness jumps off the pages when these scientists try to describe what they've figured out, shown as Fig. 9, "The Triune Brain."

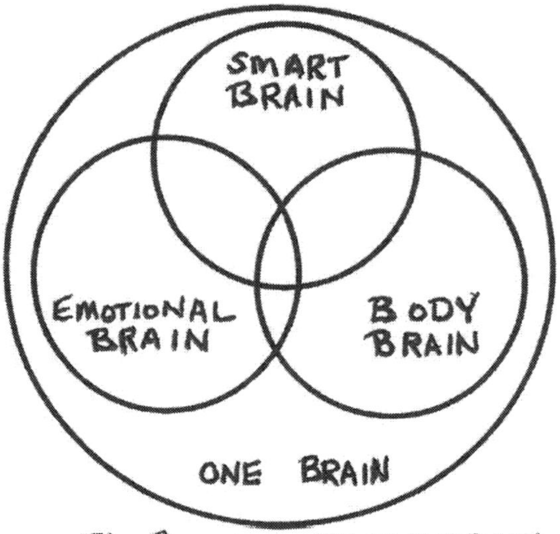

Let me paraphrase the gist of their sense of dilemma. "Well, um, there's just one brain. But it's not that simple. It's like there are three brains inside the one brain. But they aren't three separate brains; it's really one brain. We aren't sure what word to use to describe what we've discovered. The closest word that fits is that icky religious one: "Triune!"

Fig. 8: THE TRIUNE BRAIN

And I'm laughing out loud. Is that cool or what? We are truly made in God's image – God who is one God yet Father, Son and Holy Spirit in holy unity.

Here's a quotation describing the Triune human brain.

> "Each of the three levels of the brain has its own 'understanding' of the environment and responds accordingly. A particular [brain] may become dominant and override the others, depending on the…conditions. At the same time, these three levels are mutually dependent and intertwined, functioning as a cohesive whole, with the degree of integration of each level of processing affecting the efficacy of the others." Pat Ogden, Kekuni Minton, Clare Pain *Trauma and the Body*

THE THREE BRAINS

Now you know why I've been talking about:

- The SMART BRAIN (official name: neocortex or prefrontal cortex),
- The EMOTIONAL BRAIN (Also known as – AKA – the limbic brain), and
- The BODY BRAIN (AKA the reptilian brain by neuroscientists).

The whole brain works at full capacity when the Smart Brain stays in charge of the other two. The triune brain includes not just the official brain up in our skull but also the full central nervous system with tendrils that instantaneously reach to every corner of the body, every organ and every bodily system. We used to think of the central nervous system as being sort of like inanimate telephone lines that speed intel back to the brain up in the head. But, it turns out that the entire system has more active and "conscious" involvement.

EACH OF THE THREE BRAINS HAS ITS OWN "HEADQUARTERS" AND TASKS WITHIN THE FULL BODY

The **Smart Brain's** activity centers in the brain up inside the skull.

The **Emotional Brain's** activity starts in the brain but centers along the *Vagus Nerve*, a big, floppy connected strand of nerves that meanders down our torso from the lower part of our face clear to our waist. Just think about where your body registers anxiety or fear – that knot in the pit of your stomach, your pounding heart, the tightness in your throat or the sudden burning sensation when your face flushes with embarrassment. That's all done by the Vagus Nerve. And the Emotional Brain actually stores many preverbal or especially traumatic memories somewhere along the Vagus Nerve – in the nerves connected to our heart or stomach or diaphragm or throat! Isn't that incredible?

The **Body Brain's** activity centers in the extremities of the nerve endings in our arms and legs that control our posture, and the poses we adopt that wordlessly telegraph our mood or our state of mind.

Survivor Mode kicks in when Amy and Hippo alert for danger and activate the body's response.

The Emotional Brain seizes control when we flip into Flight or Fight Mode.

The Body Brain takes over when we flip into Freeze Mode.

HOW TRAUMA AND IMMATURITY AFFECT THE THREE BRAINS.

Trauma or frightful experiences can profoundly affect the development of these three brain systems. In fact, early childhood trauma, especially within the child's home, can stunt the development of the Emotional Brain which makes it harder for Pilot to develop fully.

By the way, if that's an issue, it's crucial to get counseling to work through any childhood trauma. When the Emotional Brain integrates those traumatic memories into a new resolved, healed understanding, it calms Amy and Hippo so they don't flip into Survivor Mode as much. This in turn keeps Smart Brain in healthy control as the new normal.

Emotional immaturity also goofs things up by keeping the Emotional Brain in control. Some societies actually cultivate emotional immaturity, encouraging men to give full vent to anger, supporting vendettas or feuds, setting an expectation that women will fall apart in a crisis or assuming that "good moms" will constantly worry and fret about their children.

This lends urgency to us as believers to shed old cultural props or personal immaturity, no matter what excuses we may lean on, and grow up into emotional and spiritual maturity as followers of Christ.

6. The On-Off Switch of Survivor Mode

Two analogies have helped me understand what happens when the body flips the switch into Survivor Mode: the Transformer Car analogy and the analogy of herds of animals on the African Serengeti. Let's look at these analogies one at a time.

THE TRANSFORMER CAR ANALOGY

Our brain controls all the functions in the body. It always operates under one of two, mutually exclusive modes:

- Normal Mode (AKA Parasympathetic Nervous System) or
- Survivor Mode (AKA Sympathetic Nervous System).

When I think about these two mutually exclusive modes, it reminds me of my grandson Jacob who loves playing with a little Transformer car. His little toy perfectly pictures these two modes.

His Transformer car always has the same components – wheels, car parts, side doors, etc. When he took his little car out of the packaging, it was a regular car and could function as an automobile. Four wheels on the ground support the car chassis and a little pretend driver could get in the car and drive somewhere.

But when danger threatens, all the car components instantly flip to become a Transformer "soldier" to fight against the enemy. Instead of wheels down to drive somewhere, the front wheels flip up and shift purpose. Its chassis can't do anything but deal with the threat until it flips back into a car again. Jacob's Transformer car is always either fully a Car or fully a Soldier.

In the same way, the millions of cells in the human body all operate under one set of priorities when we are in Normal Mode. All the muscles, hormones, chemical reactions and organs of the body (like heart, lungs and stomach) support Normal Mode, including the wide variety of chemicals used to recover from illness or injury, or to digest our food. But they flip into an entirely different set of priorities and configurations when Amy and Hippo sound the alarm and the body transforms itself into a Soldier.

As a handy visual, when we talk about Normal Mode, think it is as a Car with the wheels down so the car can go about its normal life. And think of the visual of the car flipping itself into a Soldier when we discuss Survivor Mode.

OK, to throw a little brain science at you, Survivor Mode is one of several **"distinct action systems"** of the brain. In their book, *Trauma and the Body*, the authors Ogden, Minton and Pain site numerous recent discoveries that have identified 8 interrelated action systems "that govern human behavior:

1. defense,
2. attachment,
3. exploration,
4. energy regulation [like eating, sleeping or wound repair],
5. caregiving,
6. sociability,
7. play and
8. sexuality."

If a person flips into the **defense** action system, it triggers the massive shift into Survivor Mode, including the activation of the sympathetic nervous system. As a Soldier, this action system sucks up all the energy making it hard to focus on anything else. The immune system in particular shuts down because it's all hands on deck to face the danger. This makes Survivor Mode unique among the eight action systems.

By contrast, a person in Normal Mode can do any of the other seven types of actions (beside defense) without switching out of the parasympathetic nervous system. So a mom, mainly in "**caregiver** mindset," can seamlessly weave in and out of **attachment,** join her children in **play** or **exploration** or **energy regulation** when she helps them eat lunch or take a nap.

On play dates she and her children can all shift into **sociability** as they interact with other moms and children. She can even handle minor safety issues, like teaching her child to stop trying to stick a fork into the electrical outlet, without herself flipping into Survivor Mode.

She would probably stay in the caregiver mindset until she finally tucks the kids in bed for the night. It would require a little bigger shift of gears to move into **sexuality** mode with daddy or into **energy regulation** when she herself falls asleep, but it's still all under the umbrella of the seven action systems at play in Normal Mode.

One last comment. I'm not suggesting that a person can't do any of the other action systems when they flip into the defense action system. A frightened person can eat, take care of children or do their job even though they're scared. In fact, people are often unaware that their body has flipped from Car into Soldier. It's just that whatever they happen to be doing outwardly to live their normal life, their body's agenda has completely shifted. The chemicals, hormones and organs have primed their physical body for life-and-death battle, not for normal life.

THE ANALOGY OF HERDS GRAZING ON THE AFRICAN SERENGETI: PART 1

All living creatures have similar SURVIVOR MODE mechanisms. It's easier to describe what happens to us by watching herd animals do it. Our body reacts in the exact same way.

1. NORMAL MODE = Herd animals having a regular day…
…walking along, eating, playing, sleeping, socializing, exploring, sticking close to mama, handling problems along the way like finding water or crossing a river. Their auto-immune system has been turned on to repair injuries. (Aha! Notice this is a fleshed out description of our seven non-defense action systems within an animal setting.)

In Normal Mode, the herd keeps an eye out for predators but has decided it's safe for now to do regular life. If a member of the herd gets in trouble it cries out for help from others in the herd, especially mama, and the herd helps it. The animals communicate to one another by their version of talking or by body language (tail flicks, color changes or facial expressions) that say all is well.

In this Normal Mode,
although they always stay alert for danger,
the herd as a whole believes:

"I'm safe enough to live my regular life."

THE ANALOGY OF HERDS GRAZING ON THE AFRICAN SERENGETI: PART 2

2. SURVIVOR MODE = The instantaneous reaction of the entire herd the moment a predator shows up.

Everyone drops what they're doing to try like crazy to escape this deadly threat. Every member of the herd fixates only on the predator. Some animals go directly into a specific survivor strategy. But, in general, after that first jolt when they spot the predator, most animals react with Plan A and then switch to Plan B if necessary.

PLAN A: Flight or Fight

Their bodies **rev up** massively to support running or fighting. Animals try to escape from the predator by running, swimming or flying away. This isn't a half-hearted stroll but a full out, 100% effort to race for their lives. If they can't escape, they turn around and attack the predator. They will do one or the other (flight or fight) as long as escape seems possible.

> During Plan A,
> the animals under attack really, really believe:
>
> "I'm not safe. I must run or fight."

THE ANALOGY OF HERDS GRAZING ON THE AFRICAN SERENGETI: PART 3

PLAN B: Freeze

If the animal concludes that it's in **immediate and inescapable danger of death** it will click into Freeze Mode, going completely limp and lifeless. Many predators are hardwired to chase an animal that runs away but they may lose interest if the animal appears to have already died. Some predators turn up their noses at eating a dead animal. So, it's a huge gamble for their prey to play dead but it's the only play left.

In Freeze Mode, the heart and lungs slow down to almost nothing, the arms and legs go lifeless, there's no reaction in the face or the eyes if the predator tries to get a rise out of it. It may appear from the outside that the animal is no longer afraid, but it actually has become overwhelmed by terror.

Freeze Mode shuts down the mind's capacity to stay present to this overwhelming terror. If the predator starts to eat the poor animal, Freeze Mode has heavily sedated it. If the predator loses interest and wanders off, the frozen animal doesn't react to their departure and stays "mostly dead" for a while just to be on the safe side.

During Plan B, the animals under attack have given up hope.
They see only:

DOOM: "I'm going to die." and
DESPAIR: "There's nothing I can do about it.
I can't move. No one can help me."

7. Survivor Mode is God's Gift

The Bible promises us that on that great Last Day when God sets all things right, He will end this deadly dance between predators and prey animals. "The wolf and the lamb will feed together, and the lion will eat straw like the ox…" (Isaiah 65:25).

But in the meantime, He has designed this incredible limbic system to protect the vulnerable and give us all a fighting chance. When we catch sight of an actual lion on the prowl, or a truck swerving into our lane, or a mugger lurking in the dark alley, our body instantly jolts us into readiness to defend ourselves or run or hide.

The more I read about the intricacies of that shift and the detail of how the body primes us for action, the more it compels me to thank God. He is an awesome Creator! God promises that "…before they call I will answer" (Isaiah 65:24). I'm convinced that by creating Survivor Mode, He has already begun to answer our cry for help in the nanoseconds before we can even get our mouth to move to form the words "Help! Help!"

This sense of gratitude and wonder has served me well lately as I explore Survivor Mode in my own body. I encourage you to adopt that same attitude. We don't need to be afraid of our body hijacking us during a crisis. If the danger is real, it's God's gift to us to allow blessed instinct to run things when our Smart Brain would maybe fatally slow us down. We can't afford to debate which door to run to if a gunman starts shooting. We need Amy and Hippo's lightning fast reflexes and lightning fast decision-making.

As someone who suffered overwhelming trauma when I was a child, I'm grateful that God created Freeze Mode. My poor little child's brain couldn't reconcile the conflict between wanting to please Daddy by being an obedient little girl and the overwhelming horror when his instruction to me betrayed my innocent trust. So God activated this mechanism that just shut it down for me. It's the same severe mercy that anesthetizes the captured gazelle so she doesn't need to stay present at her own terrifying death.

Wouldn't that be a better way to view Freeze Mode for those of us who know trauma only too well?

Most of all, I appreciate that God didn't turn Survivor Mode into a tyrant I could never escape or shut off. I love it that we can learn how Amy and Hippo's brain works and override them when they overreact. I love getting to know the unique thought processes of Body Brain. Actually, it's pretty easy to override that brain if you just know how.

And if you are willing to practice, practice, practice.

8. How to Spot when Each Brain Runs the Show

The SMART BRAIN

The Smart Brain runs the show when we are in Normal Mode. As you can see from Fig. 10, "Smart Brain in Control," all three brains work together to whatever degree of development.

Fig.9: SMART BRAIN CONTROLS

The **CENTER OF THE ACTION** for the Smart Brain is up in the brain inside our skulls where it thinks conscious thoughts and files away explicit memories.

The Smart Brain recognizes and uses the LANGUAGE of conscious thoughts or words, facial expressions and social interaction. So when Smart Brain runs the show and someone yells, "Snap out of it!" we can do just that.

You can tell that Smart Brain ran the show when something upsetting happened if:

- Your first instinct was to talk it over with a friend and talking it out resolved the problem.
- Or you thought about what occurred and debated how best to respond without spinning into obsessive or panicky thoughts.
- Or you were able to calmly discuss a huge setback at your workplace.
- Or, when your friend offended you, you frowned at them and asked, "Hey, why did you do that?" And the conversation stayed more or less calm and friendly.

The EMOTIONAL BRAIN

The Emotional Brain runs the show when we flip into Flight or Fight Mode. As you can see in Fig. 11, "Emotional Brain in Control," Amy and Hippo immediately **turn off our Pilot and <u>some</u> of our Smart Brain**. They dump adrenaline into our body and cortisol into our brain, get the heart and lungs racing, and send more blood flow to the arms and legs so we can run or fight.

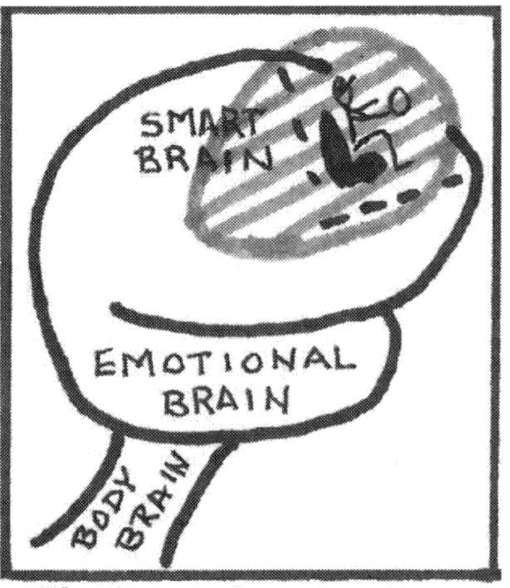

Fig. 10: EMOTIONAL BRAIN CONTROLS

When Amy and Hippo take over, they shift **THE CENTER OF THE ACTION** of the Emotional Brain to the Vagus Nerve along our torso (throat, lungs, heart, stomach, etc.). As we've mentioned before, the Emotional Brain can store memories along the Vagus Nerve itself. Mostly, these would be early childhood or even preverbal memories, or traumatic memories of any age.

Although the Emotional Brain stays hyper-alert for any verbal threat that might flip it into Survivor Mode, it mostly ignores our own mental commands trying to pull out of Survivor Mode. **Instead, it mainly recognizes and uses, as its own LANGUAGE, these bodily reactions of heart and lungs and tensed muscles that occur when the body revs up to face the threat. It also reads and interprets these unfolding reactions and body clues when deciding whether to rev up further, or to wind down, its control via Survivor Mode.**

In other words, on a conscious level, when you fully rev up into fear, panic or anger, if someone tells you to "Snap out of it!" you can't just hop to it and shut down all those bodily reactions. You may learn to hide your reactions from people so they can't spot them as plainly. But your body has a mind of its own and still reacts along the Vagus Nerve. The muscles of your arms, legs and neck stay as tensed up as ever.

And because Emotional Brain shut off your Pilot, it's likely you get swept up into the drama of the moment without much self-awareness.

The BODY BRAIN

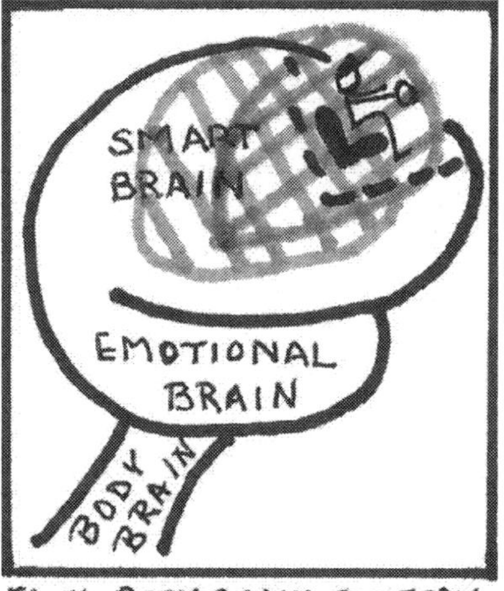

Fig. 11: BODY BRAIN CONTROLS

The Body Brain runs the show when we flip into Freeze Mode. Like a robot in a science fiction story, the Body Brain has one Prime Directive:

PRIME DIRECTIVE:
Make sure your mind survives.

If the *crisis du jour* gets too intense, the Body Brain will decide that your brain won't survive if you stay present to this time and place of such extreme danger. It pushes the panic button to shut off the brain like that robot on the spaceship that shuts down the ship's engines and sedates the crew rendering them unconscious.

When we first switched into Survivor Mode, Amy and Hippo had already shut down Pilot. But Fig. 12, "Body Brain in Control," illustrates that Body Brain shuts down <u>even more parts</u> of the Smart Brain. That's why someone in Freeze Mode will report feeling foggy or muzzy headed. The parts in the brain that recall facts and dates start to freeze up. You mentally check out and disconnect from feeling whatever is going on in your body and you lose connection with your current circumstance.

In fact, Freeze Mode shuts down a particular tiny part of the brain called *Broca's area* (named after the doctor who first noticed it). Broca's area handles your ability to form your own words or comprehend the words that people say to you.

The **CENTER OF THE ACTION** for the Body Brain is the utterly wordless body, especially the feet and legs.

The Body Brain has the most primitive LANGUAGE, which, appropriately enough is Body Language. It only understands or expresses itself through the unspoken meaning of the body's postures and poses that express its emotions at any given time.

DRAMA PRACTICE

At the workshop we did a **fun activity** that illustrates how Body Brain thinks. I led them in a simple drama exercise. We struck five or six different poses and threw ourselves into acting out each one.

- An angry Maori warrior pose with our tongues stuck out aggressively.
- A defensive pose where we crouched down and tried to block an attack from above us by our upraised, crossed arms.
- A skeptical pose with arms crossed and facial expressions to match.
- A dejected, limp and defeated pose.
- A pose of happy freedom, arms wide open, reach for the sky, legs apart and big smile.

Once we captured each pose, we closed our eyes, waited five seconds and then checked in with our body. We felt around to ask, "What do I genuinely feel right now?" In each case, the emotions in our body had quickly shifted to match the body pose.

Try it yourself. It's kind of amazing to see the immediate shift.

Freeze Mode can play out by different **degrees of frozenness**. A possum used to visit our house periodically at night. It would freeze on the fence and watch us to see if we stayed safely in the yard or tried to catch it. I would call that partial Freeze Mode. But if it had been caught by coyotes, out in the open field, it would have gone completely limp in what I would call full-blown Freeze Mode. In the same way, someone can slip into partial Freeze Mode during an argument or during a stressful committee meeting without people really ever noticing. Even in partial Freeze Mode, people will tend to lose awareness of what's going on in their own body.

It's easier to spot someone else **fully** under the control of Body Brain than to recognize when we are in its grip because, by definition, we will feel overwhelmed and disconnected. The lights are on but nobody's home. The pose will mimic the fetal position to whatever degree possible and everything will go limp and listless. The eyes won't track or react, and the body will give off a vibe that it has given up hope.

❧ ☙

Deep cleansing breath! Let's switch gears. Now that we understand more about how Amy and Hippo think when they flip us into Flight or Fight and how Body Brain thinks when it flips us into Freeze Mode, let's look at the two drills and why they work so well.

We will start with the Stand-Down Drill, explain **why** we do each part of the drill, walk through **how** to do the drill, and then summarize the drill itself.

Wash, rinse, repeat for the Grounding Drill.

9. Why the Stand-Down Drill Pulls Us Out of Flight or Fight Mode

Anybody can take some deep breaths when they're in a crisis, even without understanding the brain science on why that's so effective. I've run across many people in the past few years who had been taught some variation on this Stand-Down drill and have had some degree of success. I've even met clients who came to me for panic attacks who already did deep breathing as a management strategy.

It's been my observation, both before and after I learned this drill, that deep breathing alone doesn't work well in the long run. However, understanding the brain science behind the Stand-Down drill dramatically intensifies its effectiveness.

Remember back when we introduced Amy and Hippo? We said that there were three key actors in Survivor Mode: Amy, Hippo and Pilot. However, Pilot hadn't been developed until many years after Amy and Hippo created their database.

When we consciously direct our attention to Amy and Hippo, we help them calm down. It puts us firmly into adult mode and gives us a sorely needed sense of control and choice right when we need it most.

It also updates their database by allowing Pilot to walk through the supposed danger with Amy and Hippo. Like a good mom with a frightened child who finds a flashlight, gets down on the floor, and lets her child use the flashlight to assure himself there AREN'T monsters under the bed, Stand-Down and Grounding drills add Pilot's invaluable, calm perspective to that childhood set of fears.

Stand-Down drill is a longer ritual than mere deep breathing, but the very length of the drill does a better job of pulling us completely out of Survivor Mode and back into Normal Mode.

OK, LET'S THINK LIKE AMY AND HIPPO THINK

They activate Flight or Fight when they truly believe we're in danger. They feel they have spotted a "predator" and they remain **fixated on that danger**, doing the whole procedure of switching us into Soldier Mode, pumping out adrenaline and cortisol, etc. Until they hear otherwise, they are ON THE CASE to help us survive. They feel noble for shutting off that "slowpoke" Pilot and some of our Smart Brain.

However, they aren't rigid about staying in Flight or Fight Mode. For example, imagine we take a walk in the woods and Amy spots something on the path that vaguely looks like a snake. Instantly, she and Hippo startle and we jump back to a safer distance. But if, from that safer place, we take a second look and see that it's only a stick on the path, they breathe out a big "Whew!" of relief and readily switch us back to Normal Mode.

It's easy to stand down for a visible danger because we can tell when it no longer threatens us. But many of the potential dangers that trigger us these days are less visible and more emotional or social. The "predator" might be our boss at work, or our mother-in-law who gave us a glance we perceived to be critical, or the post on social media that sets us off.

For those more mental dangers, Amy and Hippo watch for clues within the body to decide whether to keep supporting Survivor Mode or whether they can safely disconnect. Since their "language" includes the body parts connected by the Vagus Nerve, they keep an eye on our heart rate, breathing, tensed muscles, etc. A few minutes after they sounded the first alarm they check back to see if we're still in danger. Are we still mentally behaving like the gazelle running from the lion? Do we need another shot of adrenaline?

If we're still focused like a laser on the danger out there, fully revved up and our heart and lungs continue to race, they conclude, "Oh, we must still be in danger. We need another round of adrenaline."

Boom.

But if they check back and find us breathing calmly with relaxed muscles, they conclude, "Oh, everything must be ok. We can go back to Normal Mode once again." And they switch back.

Now, here's the tricky part. That's how they think. So how can we use that to our advantage? We can't force Amy and Hippo to shut off adrenaline. We can't force our heart to beat slower or our stomach acid to stop churning. **We can only manually override two things: our breathing and our muscle tension. And we can shift our intense focus from off our "predator" to – literally – anything else.**

The Stand-Down Drill will train us to shift focus to concentrate ONLY on slowing down our breathing and then manually relaxing the muscle groups in our arms, legs and neck. It works well because it speaks Amy and Hippo's language.

Nobody can prevent the first adrenaline dump when Amy and Hippo flip us into Survivor Mode. Stand-Down Drill focuses on preventing the second adrenaline dump so our body can completely return to Normal Mode as quickly as possible.

10. Tips for Doing an Effective Stand-Down Drill

This drill has four components that work in order and build upon each other: Notice, Breath, Muscles and Calming Words. In this chapter we will give pointers to ensure the biggest and best result when you do this drill. In the next chapter, entitled "The Stand-Down Drill," we will provide a one-page summary sheet to do the actual drill.

NOTICE

This first step does three crucial things.

1) **It reactivates Pilot**. Just by noticing that your body has revved up you have already stirred Pilot to life again. Remember, Amy and Hippo compiled their "database of dangerous stuff" in early childhood, long before Pilot had formed. By reactivating Pilot to work with Amy and Hippo during this supposed danger, it helps them update their database to reflect more mature input.

2) By choosing to do a Drill instead of continuing to freak out, **it shifts the mental focus off of the "predator"** and onto the task of calming down. Amy and Hippo take it very seriously that your mind has chosen to focus on something else. In their worldview:

No longer fixated on the threat = no more danger

3) **It collects and reunifies your three brains**. The thought will occur to us to do a Stand-Down precisely at a time when we're agitated, distracted by the drama, and throbbing with all this raging adrenaline. Everything in our body screams at us to freak out about the perceived danger. And our three brains have scattered and now work at cross-purposes. So we sort of tell them, "Attention. Listen up. I've got a new job for you. Let's all focus all of our attention on our breath. OK. Go."

All three brains can do this simple task. It pulls the rest of the Smart Brain on line to do one extremely basic task. The Emotional Brain gets pulled in to breathe instead of freak out. The Body Brain shifts mood by the physical actions we take while doing the drill and it gets lulled into a calmer mindset by the rhythm and relaxation of the muscles.

One last comment before moving on. You'll notice, on the summary page for both Drills, a note that reads, **"DO THIS DRILL ONLY IF ACTUAL DANGER HAS PASSED!"** Nine times out of ten when Pilot flickers awake during a crisis time, its contribution will help you handle the crisis in a wiser way. By all means, do this drill at those times.

However, if you're running for your life to escape a wild animal, or if you find yourself in the middle of an active shooting or other life-or-death danger, for heaven's sake, don't do this drill! Let Amy and Hippo shine and do their thing to keep you safe. Don't undo their fabulous work of switching you into Soldier Mode quite yet.

BREATH

The breath holds almost magical power if we know how to harness it. People in the grip of Flight or Fight Mode will breathe faster and shallower than normal. Think about what happens when we gasp in shock. We inhale quickly and hoard that breath since we may need it. So in times of danger we breathe in, breathe in, breathe in with shallow, panting breaths. That's the breath pattern for Survivor Mode, AKA the sympathetic nervous system.

Stand-Down breaks that breath pattern in two ways.

First, we use Pilot to force ourselves to **breathe a much longer breath**. That slows down the breath. When I first teach people to do this drill, I encourage them to actually use an arm to visually start at their mouth and slowly extend out full-length during an exhale, let the arm hang there for a second or two and then follow the inhale slowly back to their mouth. Maybe mentally count to 5 out, pause, and then count to 5 back. (Using the arm to visualize each breath pulls Body Brain on board.)

Secondly, focus on **balancing the length of time for the inhale and the exhale**. Think about what happens when we realize that the danger we worried about has passed. The oncoming car *didn't* crash into us. We *passed* the test we had dreaded we would fail. The limp body we pull out of the swimming pool suddenly coughs. We react by doing a strong, deep exhale. Whew! That "Whew!" is the breath pattern that signals the reactivation of Normal Mode, AKA our parasympathetic nervous system.

I tend to do about four cycles of the BREATH step until I have established a strong rhythm and have slowed down my breathing to that calmer pace. Keep the breathing going when you add the next steps.

MUSCLES

Once the breath step has finished I begin to add muscles. In this step we focus on one muscle group at a time. Deliberately **over-tense** that muscle (on the 5-count inhale) and **over-relax** them on the 5-count exhale.

I generally do it in this order:

- **Left arm** (clenching fist, forearm, and up to the shoulder);
- **Right arm**;
- **Left leg** (all the muscles from the toes up to the hip);
- **Right leg** and then the muscles of the
- **Neck and shoulders**.

Aim to do four sets each. Then check around for any tensed spot we missed and do that as well.

The transition from doing only breaths to adding muscle groups always feels to me like when I'm riding a bike and lose my footing on the spinning pedal. It takes concentration to coordinate so my sneakers can catch up with the pedal. We coordinate the muscles to the breath, not breath to the muscles. That means that even though it feels counterintuitive, we start the MUSCLES step on the exhale of over-relaxing the left arm muscles and then over-tense them when we inhale. After that, it's easy. And again, it's important for our conscious mind to focus intently on each part as we over-relax or over-tense.

CALMING WORDS

We end this drill by using words because the Smart Brain had only been partially shut down. When we revved up into Flight or Fight we probably used plenty of harsh or panicky words to vent our worries, fears, frustrations or anger. In this last step we shift our dialog into a calmer mindset.

This phase always reminds me of what I used to say to calm down our crying babies. I used a calm tone of voice in a rhythmical way. My baby could sense my steady beating heart. In a very real sense, our Pilot acts like a good mom or dad comforting and soothing Amy and Hippo.

I always start with this simple, reassuring message and wait until the start of an inhale to begin.

- On the inhale: "It's okay to stand down."
- On the exhale: "All is well."

I will do this about four complete times and then check around internally to see if all is calm yet. Usually I find residual revved up emotion of whatever kind. So I do a cycle that inputs the good opposite of that stirred up emotion: courage for fear, peace for anxiety, wisdom instead of wildness, love for anger or hate. I use the inhale to receive the good emotion and exhale to get rid of the non-helpful emotion. Example:

Inhale: "I receive the love of Christ." (Actively imagine perfect love filling your lungs and then your entire body.)

Exhale: "I rid myself of hatred." (Actively imagine hatred getting swept out of your body and blowing away.)

You can adapt this in whatever way. I sometimes do two or three sets of calming words. Sometimes I use a calming Bible promise or healing words I've heard in listening prayer times, such as:

Inhale: The One who loves me is here…

Exhale: So all will be well.

When you have finished, be quiet and enjoy the new sense of calm. Go back to sleep if fears had kept you awake, or wash your hands and return to the upsetting meeting in a calmer frame of mind.

Since I'm a believer, I usually finish by feeling around in my spirit to sense the presence of God here in this place. God is fully present everywhere. I shift into aligning with Him, whatever that might mean in the moment. Often, I actually shift position to wherever I've sense Him here and now. Then I talk with Him about the problem at hand. The Stand-Down Drill has calmed me down but it has not removed the problem. I just can talk about it or handle it in a calmer, more collected way.

11. The Stand-Down Drill

This drill is designed to pull us out of Flight or Fight Mode. It gives our body the message (in ways it can understand) that it's safe to "STAND DOWN" so it stops dumping more shots of adrenaline into our system.

Flight: Fear, worry, anxiety, urge to run away

Fight: Anger, aggression, urge to fight

Body has "REVVED UP"	**Visible clues:**
Heart & lungs pumping faster; huge surge of adrenaline; heated up feelings; knotted stomach or other parts of chest; jumpy; dread or anxiety; fixation on the threat; more rash than normal.	Clenched fists and muscles, esp. in arms and legs, neck, shoulders, face; jittery or guarded, flushed face and body. Carotid artery shows rapid heart rate. May sense the throat choking or sudden stomach acid

DO THIS DRILL ONLY IF ACTUAL, LIFE-AND-DEATH DANGER HAS PASSED!

NOTICE	that you've "Revved Up." (That brings Pilot back on line). You can pray a short prayer before moving on if you'd like: *"Dear Jesus, help me collect myself right now."*
BREATH	4 – 5 slow, deep breaths, absorbed attention to each part of each breath & slowing the breathing down. If you can, use your arm to visualize each full breath (slow exhale, let it hang there a few seconds, then arm returning to your mouth in the long inhale). Focus on making sure the inhale lasts exactly as long as the exhale. Keep on breathing slowly during the next two steps.
MUSCLES	Deliberately over-tense and then over-relax the muscles in left arm; right arm; left leg; right leg; neck/shoulders...then wherever else you find tense muscles. Four sets for each muscle group. Over-tense on the inhale, over-relax on the exhale.
CALMING WORDS	**Like a good parent to Amy & Hippo, reassure them as you would a nervous child. Address your words to them either out loud or in your head.** Inhale: "It's okay to stand down." Exhale: "All is well." **Then, check around to see what needs to get traded to bring you all to peace? Say it and imagine it happening, such as:** Inhale: "I breathe in Your peace." Exhale: "I exhale this anxiety." **Or use calming Bible verses like these from Psalm 46:10 or 2 Timothy 1:7...** Inhale: "Be still and know..." Exhale: "...that I am God." **OR** Inhale: "God hasn't given me a spirit of fear..." Exhale: "...but of power and love and a sound mind."

12. Why the Grounding Drill Pulls Us out of Freeze Mode

A DEFINITION

The word "Ground" has many definitions but the best one for our purposes defines "ground" as "the solid surface of the earth." So **"grounding" would be the act of reconnecting ourselves to the solid surface of the earth.** The Grounding Drill pulls a person out of Freeze Mode in the most basic way by gently reconnecting him or her to the actual ground or floor underfoot.

RECONNECTING AFTER DISCONNECT

Do you remember, back on page 31, when we likened Body Brain to the robot on the spaceship that turns off the engines and sedates the crew because it decided the crew won't survive if they remain aware of this overwhelming danger? Let's think like Body Brain thinks. It totally believes you're about to die from a danger that's **imminent** (right here and now) and **inescapable** (you can't out run or outfight it). Body Brain feels only doom and despair.

DOOM: "I'm going to die."
DESPAIR: "There's nothing I can do. I can't move. No one can help me."

In that terrified state of mind the Body Brain:

- Disconnects your **Pilot** from the rest of your brain.
- Disconnects **a lot of your Smart Brain** from the other two brains.
- Disconnects Broca's area and other **language centers** so you lose your words.
- Disconnects your brain from a **basic awareness of your body parts**.
- Disconnects your awareness of this **current place**.
- Disconnects the memory of **how to move**.

In less than three minutes, the Grounding Drill manually overrides all six disconnects and methodically "turns the power back on." Unlike Stand-Down drill that ends by "talking" to Amy and Hippo, the Grounding Drill uses action instead. We calmly make our body do things designed to calm the Body Brain's primitive worldview. That fun little acting exercise we did in an earlier chapter now gets used for real. We strike new poses and do things that act like Normal Mode. Body Brain catches up to the new emotional state, then shuts off Freeze Mode to match the body's new reality.

WHY FEET BECOME THE SAFE ZONE

In the Stand-Down drill we used the **breath** to drive the shift out of Fight or Flight Mode. We set the pace by first focusing on our rapid breath to slow it down, and then by aligning the other steps to match the rhythm established by the breath. Even though we revved up to the max of feeling highly nervous, angry or upset, we could handle looking directly at our intense reactions along our Vagus nerve. We felt empowered by Pilot when we slowed our breath and consciously noticed and relaxed the muscles that had also gotten caught up in our reaction to the danger out there.

The Body Brain cannot possibly directly face any of that. All that extreme emotion, and even our raucous surges of adrenaline to combat the danger, has scared the ever-living Bejeepers out of it. And it would be worse than useless to say, "Hey, let's take a deep breath!" Body Brain has already lowered our breath rate to almost nothing.

Dude, if we breathe any slower, we'll pass out!

The feet become, quite literally, the farthest part of our body away from the fogginess of our brain and the scary emotions pulsating along our Vagus nerve. Feet feel like a safer, quieter place to the Body Brain. Plus, remember that "the center of the action for the Body Brain is the utterly wordless body, especially the feet and legs."

So, we use our feet.

This diagram summarizes the sources of healing rhythm in the two drills.

THE SOURCES OF HEALING RHYTHM IN THE TWO DRILLS

The Stand-Down Drill calms the Emotional Brain by rhythm of…	**The Grounding Drill calms the Body Brain by rhythm of…**
…the BREATH Slow, deep breath IN Slow, deep breath OUT	…the FEET …**Grounded** to the floor again and then **Moving**… Slow, focused left foot step Slow, focused right foot step

A DOG STORY ABOUT MOVING AGAIN

Let's add in another little interesting brain science factoid. In the course of studying how the human brain processes trauma, I ran across a fascinating anecdote somewhere about some lab animals. (Sorry. I couldn't track the source.)

These dogs were kept in individual cages (poor things) and got locked in every night. Every morning the lab technicians would open the cages and let them out for some free time. The dogs loved getting out and usually hopped out without a second thought.

One night a terrible storm raged and the lab got flooded. Icy water crept up into the dog cages and stayed around until morning. The pitiful dogs got tremendously traumatized. But when the lab guys opened the cages to rescue the dogs, they didn't move. They just huddled in their cages.

The lab techs figured out that during that horrible night the dogs had forgotten how to walk! They **couldn't get out all during that long night** and it convinced them in their little doggie brains that they could **never get out**. The lab guys worked with each dog and had to manually show them how to move one paw and then the other, how to stand up and how to make one new step at a time. Thankfully, the dogs developed new muscle memory and lots of treats helped them forget their fears and walk again.

Now let's apply this to humans. Most of the adults who repeatedly slip into Freeze Mode have suffered some kind of big trauma in their story. Usually, the trauma happened when they were quite young or even preverbal (like an infant or toddler). So that trauma happened when their brain development still resembled the maturity level of these fragile doggie brains. At that age they were really little and easily overwhelmed. And it was absolutely true that they could not escape back then.

That sense of **desperate hopelessness** deeply imprinted on their brain as a data entry in big red letters exactly at the time when Amy and Hippo were busily setting up their database defining dangerous stuff. Years later, Amy, Hippo and Body Brain still view any stressful circumstance that remotely resembles that Red Letter Early Trauma as a kill-switch-worthy emergency.

In exactly the same way that those poor puppies became absolutely convinced they couldn't move, **under the grip of Freeze Mode, our Body Brain has convinced itself that it can't move.** That's why we will finish the Grounding Drill by teaching our body to walk again. The BODY BRAIN needs to feel our toe muscle tighten, then our ankle clench, then all the calf muscles prepped and ready to take our first step. And then we activate each muscle on the other foot and leg to take our second step.

Body Brain convinced itself that we can't move which translated into the emotion of despair. Pilot gently teaches our feet and legs to walk again.

To physically walk = emotional hope and escape.

Body Brain's mind releases its emotion of despair once it feels and sees itself walking. It's magical to watch this transformation!

THE TRICKY CHALLENGE OF CALMING OUR FRIGHTENED "CHILD MIND"

No matter what our actual age, while in the grip of Freeze Mode, our mental age has slipped into early childhood. The Grounding Drill works well when we keep this primitive child's mind uppermost in our consideration. In this drill our Pilot acts the part of a wise, kind mom or dad coaxing a frightened child into feeling safe again.

So no judging! I mean it. No self-loathing that I'm a scared little kid. We just start doing silly stuff that arouses our Body Brain's curiosity and distracts it from its fear. A few pointers will keep our Pilot in an effective state of mind. (You'll learn the exact steps of the Grounding Drill in the next chapter so this is a spoiler alert. But it goes to the mindset that will make Grounding much more effective.)

Keep it simple enough for a four year old to do it.

- In the early steps, keep any **question** or any **instruction** simple.
- Keep **labels** simple, the vocabulary of a child who has learned names of things but can't necessarily read the words in a book. Stick to the items in this room or this place only.
- Keep the **numbers** simple. No multiplication or higher math. Stick to addition only and stick to problems with an answer of 10 or less. No asking for a phone number or an address or the square root of pi, because if we suddenly can't remember it, it will freak us out again.
- Keep it simple on **learning to walk** again, the lab tech helping the puppy dogs to walk.

Think "Goofy."

Play up the silliness of squishing toes or taking steps in a goofy way. Make a big production of sitting up straight and playact pulling up the string of your spine. (Don't worry. I'll get to that in a minute.) Turn this drill into a gentle Game as soon as possible. Smile more as you go along and give yourself credit for accomplishing each step of the drill.

Remember back when we talked about the on-off switch between Survivor Mode and Normal Mode? The newest discoveries about the eight action systems support this emphasis on goofiness. We want to pull ourselves out of the "defense" action system and back into one of the other seven systems under the umbrella of Normal Mode: attachment, exploration, energy regulation, caregiving, sociability, play and sexuality.

Since Freeze Mode has turned us temporarily into a frightened child, we cannot or should not make the jump into a few of those action systems like caregiving, sociability or sexuality. **The best and safest transition for a frightened child takes us from fear mode into play and exploration mode.** In other words, be goofy.

Lastly, memorize this drill BEFORE you need it.

Know it backwards and forwards. Practice! Practice! Practice! Three times through will not cut it when your Pilot has shut off and most of your Smart Brain knowledge has wandered away into the fog. Take it seriously that you will be at a huge disadvantage trying to ground yourself when you hit bottom. Practice this drill every morning for a month. That's the level of practice I mean. You will remember it well and it will work like a charm if you know it cold.

The Grounding Drill has five parts: Notice, Feet, Seat, Labels and Move. When I teach this drill to newbies, I always spend a few minutes teaching them a little playacting game to remember the action steps.

Memorize: FEET, SEAT, LABELS, MOVE. Repeat three times in a firm voice. FEET, SEAT, LABELS, MOVE. Say it again. Then I add pantomime motions for each step and we repeat the whole thing three times.

FEET: Fingers point to feet.
SEAT: Smack your butt.
LABELS: Point fingers of both hands to sweep this room.
MOVE: Fingers point at feet again.

It wouldn't be a bad idea to keep those four words on a 3 x 5 card or on a note in your phone. Or print out a copy of the drill to prepare in case your brain totally freezes up.

OK. Now let's discuss technique.

13. Tips for Doing an Effective Grounding Drill

Again, the Grounding Drill has five parts: Notice, Feet, Seat, Labels and Move. It normally takes about two or three minutes to do this entire drill. It's best to do it in a private place so you can throw yourself into doing the goofy parts without feeling awkward. For each step I'll include the instructions I give to a newbie on how to do this drill. When I do it for myself, I talk myself through it in the same way.

What Body Brain Disconnects	Step(s) that Reconnect Them
Pilot from the rest of your brain	Notice, Feet
Much of Smart Brain from the other two brains	Notice, Seat, Labels
Broca's area and other **language centers** so you lose your words	Labels
Your brain from a **basic awareness of your body parts**	Feet, Seat, Move
Your awareness of this **current place**	Seat, Labels, Move
The memory of **how to move**	Move

NOTICE

If any version of this thought crosses your mind, "Oh my gosh! I think I'm slipping into Freeze Mode!" congratulations, you have already activated your Pilot. (And, yes, if that thought occurred to you, you already picked up on body cues of Freeze Mode.) Have no worries that you need to do something else to activate Pilot. You can just run with it. Operate on the assumption that Pilot has joined you and together you will sort things out.

Pay no attention to the gloom and doom. It's temporary and you have a good chance of maybe altering it pretty quickly. So don't get sucked into the drama as if that's what you need to fix.

But lastly, before you move to the next step, **be kind to yourself**. If you just got tragic news and feel overwhelmed, don't do the Grounding Drill right away. Or if bullets fly and you're desperately trying to play dead, you'll sell it better while still in Freeze Mode.

On the other hand, even in times of great danger it's much better to pull yourself together so you'll make better decisions. And if it's four months after the tragedy and you struggle to pull yourself together, the Grounding Drill will help more than you can imagine.

FEET

Your brain will feel really foggy and disconnected from your body. So even before you try to ground your body to the floor you must reconnect your brain to your body. The idea of "Pilot" floats around as an abstract idea that needs to get tied to a concrete place in our body.

So, first, gently place one hand on your forehead and welcome your Pilot. Keep your hand on Pilot and look around for your feet. Pick one foot. **Focus on that foot until you can feel your foot from your foot's point of view, not just by seeing it.**

What does your foot feel?

- Hot or cold?
- Sweaty or dry?
- Roomy or cramped?
- Does anything hurt or does it feel fine?

Repeat for the second foot. By now, you don't need to keep your hand on your forehead.

Now focus all your absorbed attention on finding – and feeling – the floor. Once you reconnect with your feet, use both feet to squish around into the carpet, the flooring or the ground. Explore it. What does the floor feel like? Wait until you can sense the softness of the carpet or the solidness of the concrete or unique quality of whatever your feet rest upon.

Now push against the floor while you savor its sturdiness. I'll often end by saying, "These are my feet squishing into this floor. This floor is solid and steady."

SEAT

This step shifts our posture out of a defeated fetal position, with its limpness and dejection and replaces it firmly with a **centered, confident, open stance** that gets us ready to look at this room. I use the word "butt" deliberately for the jolt it gives and the sense of command even though I speak softer words.

I talk to myself, either out loud or in my head, recalling what to do and then doing it. "OK, now let's shift position a little bit. Move around in this chair until my butt is centered and all the way to the back of the chair."

Imagine that there's a little string like a puppeteer's string all along your spine. **Put your fingers on the back of your neck and pull up the string until your spine is as straight as can be, even a little bit facing upward.**

Do you feel it?

Now take your hands and **smooth your neck upwards until your chin's as high as you can go.**

Next rest your hands on the arm of your chair with your **palms opened upward in a relaxed position**. Be quiet for a few seconds waiting for the Body Brain to make the shift into this confident, centered, open stance. Almost always this position shift prompts a **spontaneous deep breath**. The deep breath is our clue that Body Brain has shifted.

If you do this drill from a standing position, the key is to stand up straight with shoulders back and legs comfortably apart. We do the same deal with the string, the spine and the chin, and then let your hands dangle comfortably with the palms facing upward.

Soon you will notice the room around you and it often catches you by surprise.

LABELS

Calmly look around this room and shift into naming objects you see in the room. Make it simple: bookcase, chair, lamp, door, carpet and book.

Now shift into **adding the color**: the tan rug, the white dresser, the green and blue toy, the stainless steel trash can.

Then add numbers that add up to less than 10: eight cubbies, four chairs, three houseplants, two paintings on the wall.

No pressure. Make it a game. Anything you can't recall gets a goofy temporary name for now so we can move on without falling into a funk again.

Don't draw attention to anything stress-inducing or scary. Don't focus on a clock unless you have tons of time.

I love the elegance of this step. It gives us back our words starting with the simple ones a kid would learn early on. *Broca's area* specifically holds the words that describe our emotions and so notice that we don't ask about any emotions yet. But by starting with basic vocabulary, it kind of kick starts our words, and helps *Broca's area* to loosen up a little so we can regain those words if we need them.

Plus, this step gets us looking around this room in a friendly, curious way. In fact, we study this room in far greater detail than we ever would otherwise, which neatly reorients us into this present place and time. And we never had to spell it out: "It's OK to come back because this room isn't terrifying anymore." Instead, our little name game demonstrates that it's safe and ordinary.

MOVE

Now turn your attention from the whole room back to your feet. This part works fine either with shoes on or off.

Focus your attention on one foot, specifically your big toe on that foot. Tense your toe so it points up. Do it until you can feel it tensing. Now start adding muscle groups one by one to that tensed toed. Tense the top side of your foot. Then tense up your ankle and then your calf muscles all the way up to behind your knee. If you do this correctly, you will end up with your foot on tippy toe and your entire leg, from toe to knee, braced as if you're all set to run the hundred-yard dash.

Can you feel that? Great.

Gradually relax that foot and go through the same process with your right foot. Tense up big toe, top of your foot, ankle, calf. Hold it and then relax.

Now alternate one foot and then the other as if you were making a pretend footstep. Focus all your attention on each part of each footstep. Do this for two or three full pairs of footsteps.

You are now prepared to **take some steps around the room**. Tensing the muscles will give the appearance of pushing off from a crouch to standing on tiptoe and back to a crouch again, and then rocking to the other foot from a crouch to tiptoe and down again. Start out staring intently at each part of each step which means you'll lean way over to watch your feet. For some reason, when I do this, my arms tend to extend out a little in sway with each step for extra balance.

In other words, you will look like a big gawky bird – a flamingo or Big Bird from Sesame Street™ or an egret. For the first few steps your "bird" will hunch over to focus on the tensed muscles for the leg, but within a few steps your arms will feel more expansive and you will think about leaping or flying.

By the last few steps, straighten up fully and walk upright with your arms moving freely. I say to myself, "I am free to move. To glide. To leap." Imagine your feet doing just that.

Finish the drill by returning to sit in your chair.

I've led dozens of individuals through this drill. Most of them felt defeated or discouraged or listless when we began. I have yet to find anyone who completed all the steps of this drill who didn't feel measurably more optimistic or more empowered by the end.

[As this year of experiments went along, you will notice that I added other refinements to this drill. But this will give you a good start.]

14. The Grounding Drill

This drill is designed to pull us out of Freeze Mode. OUR TASK: Gently reorient to THIS room, THIS body (especially our feet firmly grounded by THIS floor), THIS time & place, to regain our WORDS and the body memory that we can MOVE.

Freeze: Limp, numb, paralyzed, urge to give up

Body has "SHUT DOWN"	Visible clues:
Breathing & heart rate slow way down; mind feels foggy or numb & has difficulty recalling simple info normally known; feels overwhelmed and unable to act.	Body goes limp or sleepy; arms & feet dangling. Posture hunched over, curled in, dejected, no movement. Person doesn't show their normal connection to this time & place.

DO THIS DRILL ONLY IF ACTUAL, LIFE-AND-DEATH DANGER HAS PASSED!

NOTICE	...that you're in Freeze mode (Hurray! Pilot's back.) If you feel up to it, pray a brief prayer: *"Jesus, help me collect myself."*
FEET	Gently touch your hand to your forehead to find Pilot. Let Pilot focus on one foot until you can sense what those toes are feeling from the toe's point of view. My toes feel cold, hot, squished or comfortable? This connects our Smart Brain to our Toe. Do the same with the other foot. Now squish both toes to the floor and ask yourself the same questions about the floor. This floor is carpet, tile, cement, dirt? It feels soft or hard? Notice that the ground is solid under your feet. Maybe finish this part by saying to yourself: *"This is my own foot firmly planted here on this solid ground."*
SEAT	**Center** your body into full upright & confident position, butt fully back into the chair, legs centered, and shoulders back. Use a hand to gently nudge your chin up as high as it can go. Now rest your hands at your sides in a comfortable position with the palms up. Pause a few seconds until you feel the difference in that new position. You've done it well if your new pose is the literal opposite of fetal position.
LABELS	Now look around the room and play a little game with yourself. Say the name of four or five objects in this room or this place. Then name the color of four things. And then count the number of several things, such as the number of shelves in a bookcase, the number of chairs or windows or houseplants. Ask yourself easy number questions whose answer adds up to 10 or less.
MOVE	Shift your attention back to your feet again. Deeply focus on tensing the muscles in your big toe, top of your foot, your ankle, and up the calf. These are muscles you use to take one step. Do the same with the other foot. Take a few practice steps still sitting down and focus attention on each step. We remind our feet how to walk again. Then get up and start doing actual steps focusing intently on each part of each step. Gradually begin to think of yourself as leaping with each step or starting to fly. Say to yourself: *"I am FREE to move. To glide. To leap."* Lastly, do a simple task and sit back down, such as get a drink of water, clap three times, plump the pillow in the chair or whatever. Sit down and you're done. Doesn't that feel better? *"With Your help I can advance against a troop; with my God I can scale a wall." Psalm 18:29*

15. Using the Window of Tolerance to Foster Resiliency

...and one ring to rule them all.
JRR Tolkien *The Lord of the Rings*

OK, deep cleansing breath! We've learned a lot of bits and pieces about our amazing brain and Survivor Mode. Now, in this little chapter we will tie it all together by discussing an elegant concept called the Window of Tolerance (WOT), shown as Fig. 12. It's like Frodo's one master ring because everything we've discussed so far finds an application within our understanding of this diagram. When the idea occurs to us to wonder if we need to activate Pilot and do a drill, the Window of Tolerance will orient us to our present emotional state, making it much easier to figure out what to do next.

"Hair on Fire" Rage

Fig. 12 THE WINDOW OF TOLERANCE

10		
9	Emotional Brain runs the show	SURVIVOR MODE: ON
8		Flight Mode: Run or Worry
7		Fight Mode: Get angry or fight
6	**"The Window of Tolerance"**	
5	Smart Brain Runs the Show	NORMAL MODE: ON
4		
3		
2	Body Brain runs the show	SURVIVOR MODE: ON
1		Freeze Mode: Shut down

Numbness

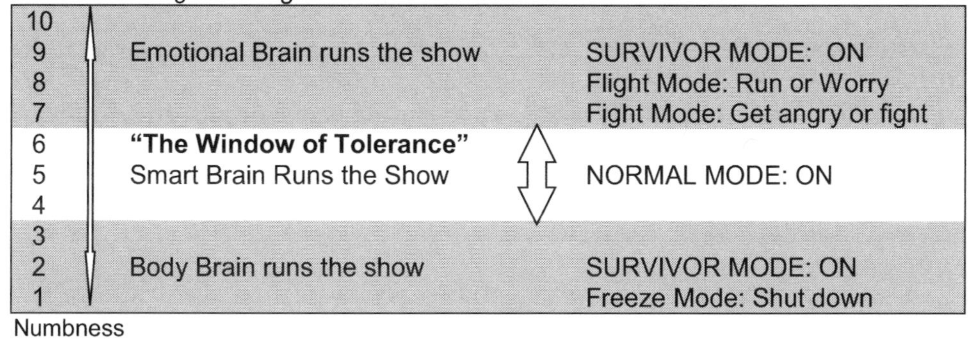

Everybody goes through a variety of changing moods and circumstances which affect how well we respond to a new possible danger. Let's start at the far left side of this diagram. You see the **numbers along the left side from 1 to 10**? These represent the range of emotions we might feel at any particular time. At the bottom, the #1 represents the most extreme paralyzed or frozen state, then less bleak for 2 and 3. As the numbers approach the center we feel more upbeat and collected. The higher numbers show our state of mind as we get more agitated by anxiety, then up to worry or anger clear up to the 10 territory of hair-on-fire level of rage.

So, first big idea: At every moment of waking life, we can always locate ourselves somewhere along the tall narrow arrow of numbers between 1 and 10. When we activate Pilot and it assesses our body cues, it will identify which number best captures our current state of mind. Have I revved up? Have I shut down? Am I staying calm? And how extreme is my reaction? Most people tend to hang around somewhere in the middle numbers unless an upsetting development triggers Amy and Hippo into firing up Survivor Mode.

The three, wide horizontal bands show the On-Off switch which has been turned on in the upper and lower shaded areas. In the middle band Survivor Mode has been turned OFF and Normal Mode is back ON.

The entire central band is also called "The Window of Tolerance" because in that zone we can carry on our normal life, even the stressful parts, without sliding up or down into Survivor Mode. In the middle zone, we can "tolerate" whatever life throws at us and still keep our head.

The white middle band = The Window of Tolerance = Normal Mode.

The big fat arrow in the middle band shows the strength of Normal Mode for each person. Everyone settles into their own version of this middle band. We can't help what our WOT looks like now. An easygoing, patient person might stay steady with a fat white band because nothing much rattles them. They don't often worry or get angry and rarely feel blue.

Habitually angry people have a small WOT because they jump up to level 10 rages at the drop of a hat. At the other extreme, so might shy or traumatized individuals since they get easily flustered, anxious or overwhelmed, sliding often either up into fear and worry, or down into discouragement or numbness.

The width of this WOT may fluctuate when we go through a bad patch. A normally steady woman might startle often right after her house gets robbed but then bounce back to normal within a few months. Or a normally anxious teenager might rise to the occasion during a crisis and keep calm and cool because the disaster demands it.

BUT NOW COMES THE FUN PART!

We can change quite a lot about this diagram if we become more proficient at pulling ourselves back into the Window of Tolerance. We have two main goals for our own Window of Tolerance: a short term goal for handling each stressful situation as it comes up and a long term goal to dramatically reshape our WOT.

Our Short Term Goal: Pull ourselves back into the white middle band of the WOT as quickly as possible.

Whatever the current strength of our WOT, we can make it stronger if we cut short the time we remain hijacked into Survivor Mode. We use the drills we just learned to pull ourselves quickly back into the WOT.

Like so.

Fig. 13 SHORT TERM GOAL: RETURN TO OUR WOT QUICKLY

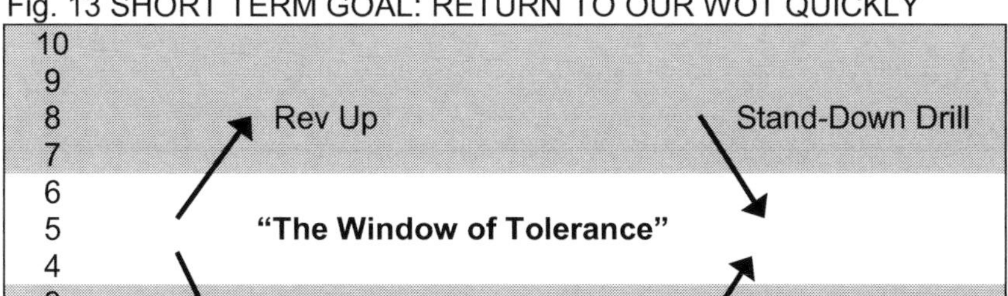

In Fig. 13, "Short Term Goal…," notice the first little black arrows that represent us Revving Up into Flight or Fight, or Shutting Down into Freeze Mode. When we notice ourselves drifting out past our WOT, we actively override that response by doing whichever drill will pull us back into the WOT.

We do this over and over again until it becomes a learned and reliable skill.

Over time, this widens our WOT because we spend less time stuck in Survivor Mode. We lose our dread of adrenaline, gaining confidence and self-control. Gradually we figure out what it feels like to stay calm and collected in the face of a wide variety of stressors and crises. This develops resiliency and emotional maturity, and sets us on the path to reach our long term goal.

Our Long Term Goal: Pursue peace, wisdom and training to widen our WOT as much as possible.

Here's the best news of all. **We can make our WOT wider** by developing good character qualities like patience, courage, optimism, and self-control. If we work on resolving traumatic experiences and build a solid foundation in our faith, that healthier perspective steadies us when new troubles hit. Our drills become one of many tools in our toolkit to achieve that goal.

Fig. 14 LONG TERM GOAL: WIDEN OUR WOT

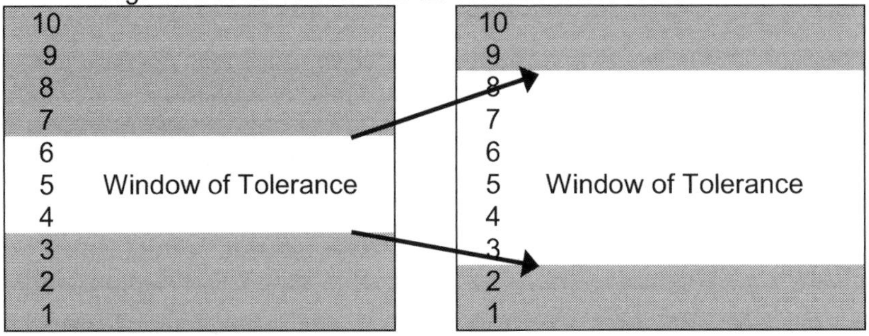

10 9 8 7 6 5 Window of Tolerance 4 3 2 1

10 9 8 7 6 5 Window of Tolerance 4 3 2 1

At my workshop, I used Fig. 14, "Long Term Goal…," to illustrate what happens when strong young adults show up at military Boot Camp. They have a pretty decent WOT to start with and a lot of cockiness that, sure, they'll act brave and bold if they ever get into combat.

The rigors of Boot Camp toughen their minds and teach them – over and over – what to do when the danger they face isn't just some little noise Amy and Hippo decided freaked them out but actual bullets and actual near-death experiences.

Boot Camp trains soldiers to stay within the WOT even during actual danger.

- The Captain who stays levelheaded when the ship takes on water has stayed within the WOT.
- The Private who shoots straight because the bullets overhead no longer distract him stays within the WOT.
- Boot Camp also teaches soldiers to manage adrenaline by discipline and a strict code of conduct.

And for us civilians:

- The mom who keeps her head when her baby gets a bad cut on his chin stayed in the WOT. She may freak out afterwards, sure, but in that crisis moment, she pushed back against the adrenaline and Pilot stayed on board helping her recall her first aid training.
- It is also the Christian who smiles into the camera filming the wreckage from the fire that wiped out every home for blocks and says, "It's ok, it's only stuff."
- And it's the Dad who stays calm and reasonable when his drama-queen teenager pitches a fit. Again.

BOOKS AND RESOURCES FOR FURTHER STUDY

I have loved studying about the brain and I hope you enjoyed this brief overview of some basics. Maybe it has given you the bug to go out and learn more. Have fun. It's so cool.

My informal studies took me far and wide to video presentations, articles, crisis management classes and many books. When I mention a few of my favorites, it does not imply that I endorse everything they say. But if you're curious, these might get you started.

Books

Caroline Leaf, *Switch on Your Brain: The Key to Peak Happiness, Thinking & Health*
Peter A. Levine, *In an Unspoken Voice: How the Body Releases Trauma and Restores Goodness*
Pat Ogden, Kekuni Minton & Clare Pain, *Trauma and the Body: A Sensorimotor Approach to Psychotherapy*
Daniel J. Siegel, *The Mindful Brain* and *Mindsight* and other books on the same topic
Bessel Van Der Kolk, *The Body Keeps the Score: Brain, Mind and Body in the Healing of Trauma*

Classes and Workshops

Billy Graham Rapid Response Team training
Critical Incident Stress Management workshops (icisf.org)
Stress and Trauma Care with Military Application (Course presented by American Association of Christian Counselors)

CONGRATULATIONS! YOU DID IT!

Now that you have all this information under your belt, let's return to our experiments for this coming year, set a few practical, measurable goals and get to work testing them out in the laboratory of real life.

3
One Year of Experiments: Three Tests

We will use three measurable tests to determine if our theory has merit

A Year of Experiments: The Three Tests

"Test Me in this," says the Lord Almighty, "and see if I will not throw open the floodgates of heaven and pour out so much blessing that there will not be room enough to store it."
Malachi 3:10

This bold challenge encourages us to test God in a good way. Here Malachi referred to tests about tithing. But this year I sense God challenging me (and us) to do tests about conquering fears and finding the peace of Christ in a significantly deeper way.

Now, I get it that this will be highly subjective, not truly scientific in the classic way. But I love the mindset of taking a huge risk to try out a new approach and evaluate it with as much steely-eyed objectivity as possible. I'm convinced God will open the floodgates of blessings as we try.

OK…Deep cleansing breath. Let's do it!

The Theory we will Test this Year

When we notice that our emotions and our physical body have slipped into Flight, Fight or Freeze Mode, if we ***first*** spend 2-3 minutes doing whichever drill best pulls us back into Normal Mode, and ***then*** pray, we will find it much easier to fully connect with Jesus and find the peace of Christ.

INDIVIDUAL EXPERIMENTS TO TEST MY THEORY

I plan to practice doing these drills at least several times a week, if only as an act of obedience, but especially whenever I feel anxious, nervous, fearful, angry or discouraged. My goal is to bring my body to peace and then see how easy it is to connect with Jesus and pray about the situation.

I plan to log the results of each attempt. Although these headers may evolve as the year unfolds, I'll start by logging these five things:

1) The Situation;
2) The Body Cues;
3) Which Drill I chose to try;
4) What Happened; and
5) What I noticed or learned.

EVALUATING THIS THEORY AND THIS YEAR OF EXPERIMENTS

It seems like my theory holds water but I haven't tested it out in a serious way. So at the end of this year, I will also evaluate the cumulative results of doing these drills over and over all year. To encourage intellectual rigor, I will evaluate the overall results using the following diagnostic questions.

MY THREE TEST QUESTIONS

1st Test: The theory itself

When I was in distress, if I did the drills *first*, did that make it measurably easier to connect well with Jesus?

2nd Test: The Short Term Goal from the Window of Tolerance

Was I able to successfully and consistently pull myself out of Flight, Fight or Freeze using the drills, even when under extreme stress?

3rd Test: The Long Term Goal from the Window of Tolerance

Was I able to widen my Normal Mode range this year so I didn't flip into Survivor Mode as often? And if I did flip, was I better able to control the degree of my reaction to avoid the extremes?

HEY, DON'T JUST SIT IN THE BLEACHERS. COME JOIN US!

By now you have all the information you need to do these drills yourself. As you can see, they're super simple, especially after you practice a bit. You'll learn fascinating and practical things about your body you never knew before.

Practice in all kinds of settings: during the night, at school, during business meetings or those heart-pounding one-on-one confrontations in the boss's office or with your mother-in-law. Try it out during an argument or, better yet, use the information to avoid an argument. Try it out when you get bad news. Add it to the routine of your quiet times of prayer and Bible study. Do it whenever you notice a body cue signaling distress.

The information you've read thus far brings you up to speed to what my fellow experimenters knew when we started our year. And as you read our log notes, they will touch on whatever we figure out later as the year unfolds. Why not write up your own notes of what you learn?

Notice the word "Experiment." I find it a much less stressful way to learn new things if I adopt a mindset of experimenting. The cool thing about doing experiments is that we learn just as much when we crash and burn as when we execute the drills flawlessly. So no stress! You have nothing to lose and many cool things to learn.

And, hopefully after you finish reading my book, feel free to continue your own research. You might enjoy reading a few of the books I mentioned earlier.

Have fun!

LASTLY, A NOTE ABOUT HOW I ORGANIZED THESE EXPERIMENTS

Relax! We aren't including 365 log entries, only the 69 entries that added new insights or puzzlements. These log notes will be presented in two formats, **chronological** and **topical**. Let me draw your attention to this sample from the January entries in the Table of Contents to point out both formats.

Jan 5	Flight Mode…And Jolted Awake
Jan 6	Freeze Mode…And Embracing our Possum
Jan 7	Flight Mode…And Nervousness
Jan 10	Freeze Mode…And the Fear of Death
Jan 11	Pilot…And Jesus our Perfect Model
Jan 19	Stand-Down…And Switching Gears

As you can see from the first column (Jan 5, Jan 6, etc.), this book is organized in **chronological** order inviting you to follow my overall evolution of insights about how to master Survivor Mode and how to let the peace of Christ rule.

I've also organized it by **topic** as you can see from the first word or phrase in the title of each entry (Flight Mode, Freeze Mode, Pilot, etc.). This book will juggle comments on a wide variety of stirred up emotions, many aspects of Survivor Mode and thoughts about many Bible verses that support this project. We could easily get totally muddled up without an overarching plan.

So my plan will label every log entry by one of eight categories you see here in bold italic. Any time the log entry theme focuses on Pilot, the Peace of Christ or the Experiments themselves, I'll label that entry ***"Pilot," "The Peace of Christ"*** or ***"Experiments,"*** respectively.

If I do a grounding drill and mainly focus on the feelings of discouragement, listlessness or numbness, I'll label it ***"Freeze Mode."*** But if that same entry highlights something I learned about doing the Grounding Drill itself, I'll label that day ***"Grounding."***

If I do the Stand-Down drill and figured out something more about the drill itself, I'll label it ***"Stand-Down."*** However, I might focus on the emotions of that day rather than the drill. If I revved up into the anxiety, fear or worry of Flight Mode, I'll label it ***"Flight Mode"*** but if the emotions revved up further into hostility, anger or rage, I'll label that entry ***"Fight Mode."***

Each log entry title will contain the clue about its focus. Make sense?

At the end of the book you'll find an **Index of Topics** in which I've grouped all the Flight Mode entries together, all the Pilot entries together, etc., including the tutorials about each. So if you struggle keeping your cool with your mother-in-law, feel free to check out all the entries for "Fight Mode." And if you have a hard time figuring out how to lower your stress level at a business meeting, feel free to check out the entries on "Flight Mode." And so on.

In addition, only in the index, I have added two extra topics, "The Brain" and "Survivor Mode," making it easier for you to go back and review the comments on Amy and Hippo, the brain itself or other basic information not specifically referred to in the log notes.

PART II

OUR EXPERIMENTS ON FINDING THE BETTER WAY TO BE SAFE

"Lord, please reveal hidden places of pain in my heart that have not known Your love.
Help me to realize that I have walls of self-protection
and help me to trust that You have a better way of making me safe."

From the Invitation Prayer we use to begin a healing prayer session

4
Silly Acts of Obedience

For the first two months
I mainly focus on mastering the drills
and ponder my new theme verse

Jan. 1: The Peace of Christ…And the Final Piece to this Experiment

THE BACKDROP

All during the previous year or so I had been doing this deep dive to study the latest neurological research on how the body processes trauma and how we can use this information to help us bounce back more quickly. It had revolutionized the way I tackled fears. And all along it had been easy to apply it right away to challenges faced by me or by my clients. I sensed that we had just scratched the surface of how to put this info to use. To that end we were planning for the workshop I mentioned. And we planned to launch the supporting Bible study the following Tuesday.

Against this backdrop of gearing up for my workshop, coming up fast in 12 days, I took my normal New Year's Day prayer retreat where I get my marching orders for the coming year.

MY NEW YEAR'S DAY PRAYER RETREAT

I sensed God's blessing over this whole project – the workshop and the experiments. He reassured me that He has stirred these plans and will bless this coming year of "Holy Experiments."

Then He added a new element that kicks it up a notch. Out of all the verses I plan to mention during the workshop, I get the sense that I personally need to sit in one verse all year:
Colossians 3:15.

**Let the peace of Christ rule in your hearts,
since as members of one body you were
called to peace. And be thankful.**

I took that to mean that during this entire year, I should meditate on this verse and actively apply it as my #1 priority every day. When troubling or confusing situations came up throughout the year and I asked God for guidance, I got the idea I should start my search for an answer at that verse and then look at the rest of this chapter of Colossians 3. Then go from there if necessary.

I'm not sure if I can explain it, but I also sensed a solemn urgency – kind of a "You ***really*** need to hear Me on this!" – that He wanted me to do these drills often. He would consider them an act of prayer and as acts of obedience.

I should do the drills even when I wasn't particularly stirred up one way or the other.

Practice! Practice! Practice!

Although I already know them well enough to teach them with confidence at the workshop, I sensed this urgency to keep doing them all year – for Him – because He had a lot more to teach me through them.

Fig. 15: FINDING JESUS

I thought about Colossians 3:15 and new ideas began to flow, related to Fig. 15, "Finding Jesus," one of the basic cartoons I planned to use during the workshop coming up in a few weeks.

Secular groups that teach this coping strategy include only the two "me" figures. **Jesus helped me to more fully sense the power and the certainty of His presence with me in that stressful moment.** When we do a drill to pull out of Flight, Fight or Freeze, we make it easy for our Pilot to find Jesus up there at our side. As I pondered this, He gave me two new insights.

1st insight: The Jesus in that diagram is there particularly as the God of Peace.

He is the best of parents to us when we flip into Survivor Mode. No earthly parent can interpret the clues correctly every single time their children get swamped by fear and anxiety. All kids mess up frequently. Even a wonderful mom may yell at a child who acted out of fear this time, not naughtiness. Most babies cry and fret at bedtime. Parents may unknowingly ignore this latest cry for help because it's such a nuisance to check on the baby in the crib one more time.

But Jesus is not like that.

He can tell the difference between crankiness or rebellion and a visceral fear response. Ephesians 4:29 urges us as Christians to edify each other **according to the true need of the moment**. More than any earthly person, He absolutely knows how to do exactly that because He always knows in each moment what we actually need. As I pondered my simple little diagram of Jesus standing alongside Pilot, I saw that in that moment when we struggle to pull ourselves out of a fear response, that Jesus perfectly understands our situation.

He shows up for us there as the God of Peace, not as the Judge of the Whole Earth or the Holy One of Israel or the Ancient of Days or the Most High, although He is all those names. In our small battle to pull ourselves out of Survivor Mode, He shows up for us as this perfectly calm and gentle God of Peace. And Colossians 3:15 invites us to get to know God specifically as the God of Peace. We will learn much more about how to find the peace of Christ if we get to know Him as that name.

The peace of Christ is more than just a matter of calming our emotions or soothing anxiety. I sense an invitation to truly get to know this aspect of God's character.

I wonder how this will work. Well, I thought, it's pretty easy for Jesus to stay at peace up there in heaven. And He is God, after all, so peace would be pretty easy for a powerful, all-knowing God to pull off. On the other hand, I'm a frail, easily daunted human, sometimes at the mercy of Survivor Mode.

Then I remembered that Jesus took on a human body with a human brain like ours which includes the limbic system that controls Survivor Mode. He, too, got adrenaline surges from time to time, just like me. He faced every temptation that comes our way yet without sin.

I welcome this invitation to focus on getting to know the Son-of-Man side of the God of Peace. How did the boy Jesus stay at peace? What factored into His perspective that kept His human side calm during emotional turmoil or relational upset?

He has called me to peace. How do I live out that calling? Every time I run to Him, all upset, my upset never disturbs His peace. He always views my *crisis du jour* with serenity that calms my fears. What exactly is it that keeps Him at peace about my story? What would keep my heart at peace if I adopted His perspective?

2nd Insight: The great antidote to Flight, Fight or Freeze is a deeper knowing of the God of Peace, not just with head knowledge, but in the visceral trenches with our reactive body.

When someone flips into Survivor Mode, Jesus is right there as the God of Peace. He's tuned to our deep need and patient to calm our fears and distress. He understands what we're going through and knows what will help us. Like a skilled doctor or nurse who doesn't get flustered in emergency situations, Jesus stays calm and collected at all times. And like the best of counselors, He knows how to calm our panic and teach us how to develop a mindset that stays calm in the midst of chaos.

Reading all the books about how the brain processes trauma, I can get intimidated by the aura of expertise they exude. This year we will be plunging into the deep end of the pool of hijacked emotions and deep-rooted fears, tackling the iron grip Survivor Mode holds over us. It's easy to get discouraged in the face of all that.

In Psalm 34:4, David testifies that: **"I sought the Lord, and He answered me; He delivered me from all my fears."** Yes, Survivor Mode holds enormous power. But Jesus is here with us as the God of Peace, modelling the exact opposite of fearful upheaval, wielding superior power that delivers us even from these fears. And He would love to teach us how to "do peace."

These two insights fill me with awe and gratitude for the reassurance that when I do these experiments this year, that God's presence will take the form of the God of Peace. I don't have to be afraid to seek Him out. He will understand when I'm afraid and help me collect myself without giving me grief about it.

I can't wait to see what You will teach me – and teach us – this year!

Jan. 5: Flight Mode...And Jolted Awake

SITUATION

I got super revved and jolted awake before dawn this Friday morning, unlike my normal sleep pattern. High anxiety all focused on the last minute details preparing for the workshop coming up – Yikes! – one short week from today.

BODY CUES

Racing thoughts, rapid heart rate, butterflies in my stomach, wide awake.

DRILL: Stand-Down

WHAT HAPPENED?

It lowered my breathing level. My body calmed down and then I felt the presence of Jesus in front of me, as if face to face. After I finished the breathing, it felt right to give my concerns to Him, to transfer them to His shoulders. *I cast my cares on You because You care for me.*

RESULT

I was able to calm my thoughts down and it felt good to give my worries to Jesus. Afterwards, I went back to bed and quickly fell asleep again. The whole experience took maybe ten minutes.

Jan. 6: Freeze Mode...And Embracing our Possum

SITUATION

During a session with a client who has a default habit of going into Freeze Mode, I got a download of insight that I shared with her. It spurred her thinking and the two of us had several *Aha! Moments* together. I'll call her Betty but, of course, that isn't her real name.

INSIGHTS

In the wild, God has given animals some basic survival strategies as His gift. Rabbits do Flight Mode by dashing away, badgers immediately attack in Fight Mode, and opossums immediately go into Freeze Mode.

For humans, many "possums" got that way because of an unbearable childhood trauma. Or we might not have had any obvious trauma but we're just naturally hard-wired to be shy and easily daunted by crowds or people who throw their weight around. In either case, if we can accept that we're a possum, and aim to become a **redeemed possum,** we can learn how to master the Freeze moment.

I've already commented on the possum who used to visit our back yard and how she could moderate her level of frozenness, depending on the level of danger. As human *possums*, we can learn to do the same. Plus, we can become a "redeemed possum" by preparing ahead, the same way we get ready for other kinds of disaster.

Betty asked, "Where are the sandbags to collect? What do I collect to weather the storms of life?"

Great questions. We practice these drills to prep the "sandbags" we'll need in a crisis. It reminds me of another client of mine who was prone to panic attacks at committee meetings. So we prepped by putting together one-page cheat notes of terms and data points she'd need to recall in her meetings. Meetings still make her nervous, but she stays more collected because she has prepared some "sandbags."

The big idea is to embrace the mode, and learn how to bend with the wind instead of breaking.

I talked with Betty about these holy experiments we're doing this year. They will give us tons of data. Practicing the drills gets us ready. Embracing our default mode – being grateful for it instead of ashamed of it – encourages us to make the best of it instead of staying enslaved to it.

Grounding Drill gives us the opportunity, over and over again, to "preach the gospel" to our body while we're in Freeze Mode. After a while, our body can develop a range of reactions, just like that possum in our back yard who could assess different situations and respond appropriately.

Then Betty commented that our conversation reminded her of the armor of God: "…and with your feet fitted with the readiness that comes from the gospel of peace" (Eph. 6:15). The "feet fitted" can speak particularly to Freeze Mode where our feet are the center of the action. The word "fitted" suggests a personalized strategy, the right shoes for the right occasion. The idea of "readiness" speaks to practice, training and flexibility, of experimenting until we master the skills.

In these verses, we don't preach the gospel of peace to the devil or to other people. We preach the gospel of peace to ourselves, and specifically to our feet. Satan uses fear and deception to shut us down and fool us into giving up. By embracing our "possum" persona and working to master it, we teach our feet to walk again and stay mobile in crisis.

Jan. 7: Flight Mode... And Nervousness

SITUATION

Nervousness preparing for the workshop, which kept me awake tonight.

BODY CUES

Lots of muscle tension. It's difficult to breathe deeply because of a strong urge to cough. Nervousness about the upcoming workshop and the worry I'll get a cold and my voice will give out. Racing thoughts.

DRILL: Stand-Down

WHAT HAPPENED?

I noticed when I worked on muscles, that I held tension mainly in my neck this time. I wondered why and got quiet to let my neck give me the answer. It felt like I was carrying the workshop prep all by myself even though Susan, Kayla and the team are doing a great job. When I finished the drill and prayed to Jesus, it felt appropriate to give that burden to Jesus to carry, instead of me. I heard reassurance: "I am here with you. I will not forsake you."

Doing the drill and then listening to Jesus calmed me way down. I read for a while and fell asleep.

INSIGHT

I hadn't noticed before to **watch for *where* my body holds tension**. It was curious to notice that the tension centered in my neck for a pretty logical reason. I wasn't consciously aware of what my body was "thinking" emotionally until I did the drill.

I felt calmed by doing the drill, especially by first over-tensing and over-relaxing my neck muscles before I prayed about what the neck tension might signify. That made it pretty easy to take that specific worry or state of mind to Jesus and find peace.

Jan. 10: Freeze Mode...And the Fear of Death

THE SITUATION

Early this morning I had two nightmares that eventually woke me at 5am.

The first was a long, drawn out nightmare in which I was at the mercy of ruthless villains who regularly brutalized me and others in every horrible way imaginable. I couldn't defend myself or protect anyone else. I felt terrified and defeated.

In the second nightmare, I dreamt that Jim had to drive our car on a narrow road that forced us to drive dangerously close to the edge of a cliff. He had an unavoidable accident. I got caught in a loop reliving again and again that long, terrifying plunge to our death. Again, nothing I could do about it.

I woke in definite Freeze Mode, gripped by the dread of death, especially my death and Jim's death, and had a hard time getting back to sleep.

A cloud of residue from the nightmares clung to me as I got ready for the new day. The dreams rattled me and it was hard to do a drill that morning. I happened to have a healing prayer appointment that morning, so I did the drill and prayed before my client arrived.

DRILL: Grounding

INSIGHT & TAKE AWAY

Jesus was very present and tender with me. He reassured me that He alone holds the power over the day of my death and the manner of death for Jim and for me. I can trust Him.

In a broader sense, this felt like one of those terrifying ***"What If?"* scenarios** that can plague us. It's hard to trust God for all the gruesome scenarios that come to mind. **He brought my heart to peace with the comfort that He already knows the manner of my death and I only have to trust Him for the one actual death He has chosen for me...and for Jim.**

The fear of death is one of the most powerful weapons in the enemy's arsenal to throw us off our game of letting the peace of Christ rule. In fact, it's one that Jesus specifically tackled for us according to Hebrews 2:14, 15:

> Since the children have flesh and blood, He too shared in their humanity so that by His death He might break the power of him who holds the power of death – that is, the devil – and free those who all their lives were held in slavery by their fear of death.

Here are a few examples of our God of Peace knowing the exact details of how someone will die, first Peter and then Simeon.

PETER: "Very truly I tell you, when you were younger you dressed yourself and went where you wanted; but when you are old you will stretch out your hands, and someone else will dress you and lead you where you do not want to go.' Jesus said this to indicate the kind of death by which Peter would glorify God" (John 21:18, 19).

SIMEON: "Now there was a man in Jerusalem called Simeon, who was righteous and devout. He was waiting for the consolation of Israel, and the Holy Spirit was on him. It had been revealed to him by the Holy Spirit that he would not die before he had seen the Lord's Messiah. Moved by the Holy Spirit, he went into the temple courts. When the parents brought in the child Jesus to do for Him what the custom of the Law required, Simeon took Him in his arms and praised God, saying, 'Sovereign Lord, as You have promised, you may now dismiss Your servant in peace. For my eyes have seen Your salvation…'" (Luke 2:25-30).

Since this happened two days before my workshop, I couldn't help but wonder if it hadn't been an attack of the enemy to throw me off my stride by humiliating me through my own Freeze Mode. Those thoughts of doom and despair used to dominate my mind for years before He helped me find healing and recovery. The attack that the enemy meant for evil created an occasion for God to give me huge comfort that enabled me to embrace the victory of Jesus over death in general and over my personal fear of death.

Jan. 11: Pilot...And Jesus our Perfect Model

The Spirit searches all things, even the deep things of God. For who knows a person's thoughts except their own spirit within them? In the same way no one knows the thoughts of God except the Spirit of God. What we have received is not the spirit of the world, but the Spirit who is from God, so that we may understand what God has freely given us…for,
'Who has known the mind of the Lord so as to instruct Him?'
But we have the mind of Christ. I Corinthians 2:10b-12, 16

BODY CUES

Nothing out of the ordinary so today is a practice day where I just pick a drill at random.

DRILL: Stand-Down

INSIGHT & TAKEAWAY

I've been noticing that some people have a hard time finding the part of their brain that embodies this calm, assessing, curious and kind persona. Partly this stems from trying to learn a new skill. And, I suspect, some of the difficulty may come from the fact that when we take the time to listen in on our private dialog, the loudest voice in our head sounds harsh and self-critical.

This morning, after I completed the drill, I sat quietly before the Presence of Jesus; His Presence steadied and calmed my heart. He is always quiet as if nothing could ever disturb His love for me or His control over the outcome. I noticed that He models all these attributes in the way He interacts with us when we're afraid. **When we step back and up into Pilot, we find Him already there. And He is already *being* and *doing* for us what we want our Pilot to learn to do.**

CALM: He doesn't enter in to our freak out but exudes peace and steadiness. He's our Rock and our Refuge. He calms by just being there, often without any words. "The name of the Lord is a fortified tower; the righteous run to it and are safe" (Proverbs 18:10).

ASSESSING: The Holy Spirit already gently searches our hearts to know our need of the moment. I had never made the connection before to these verses from I Corinthians 2, but they perfectly describe what we'd like our Pilot to do for us. How blessed we are to carry within us the treasure of the mind of Christ to help us assess in a wise way.

CURIOUS: This may seem an odd attribute to assign to Jesus because when we're curious, it's usually because we don't know something, and we're interested to figure out more. I see Jesus as curious in that He cares about us and He's genuinely interested in the details of our small lives. He isn't aloof. In the Gospels He often asks people questions – not because He doesn't already know the answer – but because He engages with people who seek Him out. For example:

"Jesus stopped and ordered the [blind] man to be brought to Him. When he came near, **Jesus asked him**, 'What do you want Me to do for you?'" (Luke 18:40).

"When Jesus saw the [invalid] lying there and learned He had been in this condition for a long time, **He asked him**, 'Do you want to get well?'" (John 5:6).

"**Jesus asked the boy's father**, 'How long has he been like this?'" (Mark 9:21).

KIND: The presence of Jesus radiates this kindly, loyal love. The old-fashioned word for it was lovingkindness. When we're most afraid and broken, He is most gentle and kind. He doesn't "dump the truck" on us when we've been hijacked by fear. We're the shrill ones, filled with self-loathing. Not Him. He calmly gives us practical help. He gives us wisdom "without reproach" when we ask for it (James 1:5).

"A man with leprosy came and knelt before Him and said, 'Lord, if You are willing, You can make me clean.' Jesus reached out His hand and touched the man. 'I am willing,' He said, 'Be clean!' Immediately he was cleansed of his leprosy" (Matthew 8:2, 3).

Jan. 19: Stand-Down...And Switching Gears

Come to Me, all you who are weary and burdened, and I will give you rest. Take My yoke upon you and learn from Me, for I am gentle and humble in heart and you will find rest for your souls. Matthew 11:28, 29

SITUATION

I had brunch with a good friend. Although I loved the visit and enjoyed catching up on the news, it stirred up plenty of emotion and bittersweet memories. Afterwards, my brain was on major overload but needed to switch gears quickly to mentally prepare for a challenging appointment with a client in the afternoon.

BODY CUES

Mainly scattered thoughts, hyped up, mind racing, triggered on several levels because it brought up some painful memories, heart racing.

DRILL: Stand-Down

INSIGHT

Stand-Down really helped me collect myself. By the end of the drill, I felt the tangible presence of Jesus and talked things over with Him. The visual that came to mind was of Jesus in Matthew 11:28-30 so I gave the "wad of mental stuff" to Jesus to hold for me. I released my friend and her story to Jesus. That gave my heart peace and relief because He carried the heaviness and gave me rest.

I had the sense of **two pieces of advice** from Jesus.

First: The problems my friend and I discussed were not my task to solve. I could pray for her but leave it to Jesus and other people to solve those problems. I shouldn't fret about it – Duh! I shouldn't fret anyway – but especially in this case I didn't need to fret because they will handle it.

Second: The Stand-Down Drill worked well to temporarily corral all my reactions to the lunch visit and put them in a "lock box" temporarily until after my appointment. But I needed to go process my stirred up reactions in more detail before the Lord as soon as possible. That lock box was designed as a temporary solution only. Reactions that intense should get resolved, not stuffed.

The afternoon appointment went well and I gave the client my full attention. That evening I spent more leisurely time before the Lord to sort out how my brunch date had affected me and got it settled in my spirit more completely. I also talked the day over with Jim and that helped enormously as well.

Jan. 20: Fight Mode…And the Meditation of My Heart

May these words of my mouth and this meditation of my heart
be pleasing in Your sight, Lord, my Rock and my Redeemer.
Psalm 19:14

SITUATION

Jim had gone to the office this Saturday morning leaving me alone to catch up on housework. While walking around the empty house doing laundry, I got into an agitated state by conducting an angry and lengthy imaginary conversation with someone who rubs me the wrong way.

BODY CUES

Angry and upset. Angry thoughts that got caught up in an obsessive loop going over and over in my mind how I would word it if I spoke to the person.

DRILL: Realized I should do Stand-Down but didn't do it.

WHAT HAPPENED

I suddenly noticed how angry I was. It jolted me into activating Pilot. Just realizing that I was stoking anger so pointlessly helped me to let go of the thought and I switched into thinking about something else.

However, it would have been wiser – especially since I was alone, with privacy and time – to have done the Stand-Down drill and addressed it full on because my grumpiness didn't go away completely. Later on that evening I acted grouchy with Jim for no good reason.

The Holy Spirit convicted me by reminding me of the rest of Col. 3:15: "Let the peace of Christ rule in your hearts **since as members of one body you were called to peace**…."

INSIGHTS & TAKE AWAY

I noticed that when I'm less revved up (at the *Flight* mode level of upset, not *Fight* mode) I'm more willing to humble myself by doing a full drill. But when I revved up further and got gripped by anger, I strongly resisted doing Stand-Down because I felt my criticisms were entirely justified. *Hmmm.*

Jan. 23: Grounding...And Three Stories

ANN'S STORY

I've been practicing the Grounding drill mainly at night. I would wake up worrying about something. After attending the workshop I noticed I was going into Freeze Mode at night. I became aware I was starting to shut down.

The Grounding drill has been helping.

One night, I got to the "Labels" part of the drill and got the thought, "I bet the devil would hate it if I gave thanks for these things I see around my room."

So I did and fell back to sleep.

LISA'S STORY

I was in a stressful meeting when it suddenly occurred to me, "I'm shutting down! Oh my gosh!" I immediately focused on wiggling my toes and looked around the room mentally naming the things in the room. It helped me collect myself.

KAREN'S STORY

I went to the workshop and learned the drills a few weeks before going in for brain surgery and then a stay in the hospital. I did the Grounding drill often. It really helped; it especially helped me stay connected to a sense of control.

Jan. 24: Fight Mode…And Anger When People Don't Agree with Me

SITUATION

It was late at night. I was tired and irritable, which led me into a dumb little tiff with Jim. I resisted letting it go because I felt convinced I was right. Later when I prayed about it, I realized that what triggered my stubbornness was my frustration: "You're not hearing me. You're not seeing my good idea." I hate, hate, hate the feeling of being misunderstood.

Eventually we worked it out, made our apologies, and came to peace, after which I journaled about it in listening prayer. I don't argue all that often with Jim, and less so since starting this focus on Col. 3:15.

CUES

Agitated, tired, argumentative, defensive, really revved up.

DRILL: Did Stand Down afterwards before I started to debrief in prayer.

WHAT HAPPENED?

Doing the Stand-Down drill really helped me relax and clear out any remnant of upset. It worked like a **reset button**. Then journaling helped me track down why I got triggered by that scenario and overreacted.

Jesus was kind to me and helped me sort things out. He helped me remember the true source of my righteous anger, years ago when my parents wrongly ignored and twisted what I said when I felt driven to speak the truth about the abuse. He reminded me of how I eventually got closure. Then he helped me to separate out that Jim is not at all like them and the tiff tonight was not a reenactment of that childhood outrage.

I sensed the Lord's reassurance that I can let it go because the actual truth – in my childhood and today – is known and seen correctly by God. I began hearing in my head the phrase from Colossians 3, "Rid yourself of…anger…."

In my spirit I sensed this from Jesus: **"Trust Me that you will find peace if you allow others the freedom to not agree with your good idea, even if it doesn't seem fair. Nothing of your integrity is harmed if you give it your best shot and then let it go. I have called you to peace. It will make Me proud of you if you choose peace."**

INSIGHT & TAKE AWAY

It reassured me to realize that I can safely pursue peace instead of pursuing the elusive and frustrating goal of trying to get everyone to agree with me. I took His promise to heart that **"Didi, you can let it go because it is known and seen correctly by Me."** If my idea is right, He sees that I'm right. If I'm actually not right, it gives me an off-ramp to stop harping on something that's not really a hill to die on.

Long ago I had sorted out that urgency to be understood and had come to peace as it related to my childhood stuff. I hadn't seen before how much that longing interferes now when I find myself in the occasional argument.

I'm an idea person and a world class brainstormer. I have tons of good ideas. I also work hard to speak the truth in love when I feel led to speak up. Sometimes we must be courageous to speak truth even when it hurts someone. "Faithful are the wounds of a friend" (Proverbs 27:6 NASB). But Jesus clearly prioritizes relational peace over arguing non-stop until I persuade everybody to my point of view.

Jan. 27: The Peace of Christ…And Hiddenness

And God raised us up with Christ and seated us with Him in the heavenly realms…. Ephesians 2:6

SITUATION

No particular trigger. I just want to sit quietly and listen to Jesus. I was troubled by distracting thoughts and interference so I went to a quieter room and closed the door. My thoughts were still all over the map.

CUES

Scattered thoughts, and heart rate higher than usual, but a pull to go spend time with Jesus.

DRILL: Stand-Down

WHAT HAPPENED?

The drill made it much easier to calm my thoughts and I sensed the presence of Jesus as the God of Peace. I sat quietly and enjoyed His company. After a while, the phrase from Col. 3:3 came to mind, "…your life is now hidden with Christ in God…."

INSIGHT

It felt like a teaching moment, "the Holy Spirit preaching to my spirit" as Martin Luther used to say. This place of hiddenness is the place of peace, not just for my pre-frontal cortex, but more importantly, for my spiritual self, my new man vs. the old man. I sensed how the activation of my Pilot and doing the drill settles my body so the more important connection gets made in the spirit.

I wondered what it meant to be hidden in Christ.

"It is hidden even from you," I heard.

I had the thought to allow the unknowing to be there. It's outside of time and space, in the unseen but real *heavenlies* of Ephesians 2:6. We set our minds on "things above," which orients us to that spiritual self already hidden with Christ, waiting to be revealed.

Jan. 28: Grounding...And Discouragement

SITUATION

Weariness swept over me. I felt discouraged about an especially difficult prayer session with a client and kept playing it over in my head. Doubts crowded in about my personal prayer times and I felt like I sure don't know how to pray well. Should I do it a different way? My heart sank because I have another challenging healing prayer appointment tomorrow.

BODY CUES

Listless, sleepy, discouraged, low heartbeat, hunched over.

DRILL: Grounding

WHAT HAPPENED

I sensed the gentle presence of Jesus and felt energized to talk it over with Him. The thought flitted through my head that I should stop watching a certain television series that I tried out last night. It was suddenly obvious that it wouldn't edify me. I recognized the convicting voice of the Holy Spirit without any harshness about it.

Jesus comforted me quietly (using phrases from Matthew 11:15 and 13:16), saying that there was no need to second-guess or feel dissatisfaction, especially about how I connect with Him. "You perceive Me through your ear. Much is hidden, as if you were blind but you hear acutely. Do not allow Satan to stir self-loathing or envy.

"I say instead, to you, Didi, 'She who has ears to hear, let her hear.' And 'Blessed are your ears that hear....'"

INSIGHT

Doing the Grounding drill woke me up and helped me connect in a practical way with Jesus. It also alerted my spiritual senses, especially my gift of discernment that had been lulled into watching a morally twisted TV show the night before. It was like I woke up and saw the danger. I have noticed the increase of programs where the "hero" would have been the villain in former decades. We get lulled into rooting for a sinful person doing sinful things because we've come to like him. (It's why I stopped watching a few popular shows and don't start watching others.)

It also alerted me to the subtle accusing whispers of the enemy to cast doubts on the very gifts I love the most. I love that the Lord opened my ears to hear His voice. **The monks in the Middle Ages knew this enemy attack well and dubbed it *The Noon Day Demon* because it tries to cut us off at the knees by ridiculing the uselessness of our calling.**

"No one will be helped by you praying for hours up here in your stupid little prayer cubicle." And "You're not doing it right" on a day when you're just slogging it out.

It disturbs my peace of heart to second-guess the most precious part of my walk with God, and doing the Grounding drill helped to settle that worry. When I talked it over in prayer, it reminded me of the *Noon Day Demon* and as soon as I spotted that slimy weasel, the jig was up.

Thank You, Jesus!

Feb. 6: Grounding...And Waking Up

With Your help I can advance against a troop;
with my God I can scale a wall. Psalm 18:29

SITUATION

I had a horrible night because I was doing a 24-hour medical lab test that really disturbed my sleep. Woke with a headache and found it hard to focus on my quiet time. Felt daunted because I had set aside this day to prepare the documentation to send off to our tax guy.

BODY CUES

Extreme fatigue, headache, lethargy, bummed in spirit with no motivation or energy.

DRILL: Grounding

WHAT HAPPENED?

NOTICE: Accessed Pilot easily.

FEET: I felt pretty grounded to the floor already so it was easy to connect Pilot to my toes.

SEAT: It really helped when I sat up in a chair in a grounded, more centered stance. I was shocked how much it helped me get more alert.

LABELS: My smart brain was already on line. I just felt exhausted, not foggy.

MOVE: The *move* portion totally shifted my mindset. Apparently, it did my brain a world of good to remember I have muscles and can move. When I got up and began focused steps around the room, my mind gravitated to saying the breath prayer from Psalm 18:
"By my God…I can scale a wall."
"By my God…I can scale a wall."
"By my God…I CAN scale a wall."

INSIGHTS & TAKE AWAY

It surprised me how well the Grounding Drill worked when I wasn't shut down in Freeze Mode but just had garden-variety morning exhaustion. I've noticed that someone in actual Freeze Mode needs all four steps to bring all parts of their brain back on-line. The FEET and LABELS steps help especially to reactivate their Smart Brain. And I was familiar with how those steps feel when Smart Brain isn't active. But this time my Smart Brain was already active which is why I moved on quickly to the next parts of the drill.

It also felt great to use Psalm 18:29 for grounding. Note to Self to use that from now on. It affirms my own capability to move and reassures me that God is here empowering me to do those daunting tasks.

I will definitely choose the Grounding drill again on sluggish mornings.

I finished my quiet time and energetically tackled the taxes.

P.S.

A few months later I went back and checked the wording of Psalm 18:29 and realized that my spontaneous cadence that morning had blended wording from two versions: the New International Version and the New American Standard Version. "By my God" is NASV and "I can scale a wall," is NIV.

It's a curious thing. I memorized a truckload of verses in King James Bible when I was a child up into my teen years. Then I switched to NASV in late teens and memorized many verses from it into my thirties. Then I switched to New International Version and have stuck with that.

So after the Lord opened my ears to hear His voice in 1999, since I know a ton of verses, He often speaks through Bible verses. And when I feel led to go back to revisit a traumatic memory so He can heal its pain, His healing words often includes an appropriate Bible verse or phrase. And, get this, He will use the wording of the version I was using when that traumatic event happened. Isn't that odd?

Actually, I find it comforting that He knows me with that much attention to the details of my story.

So I don't feel too bad mashing the two since all three versions have burrowed so deeply into my soul and apparently He doesn't mind using all of them.

Feb. 8: Grounding...And Silly Acts of Obedience

Then lie on your left side and put the sin of the people of Israel upon yourself...for 390 days.... Ezekiel 4:4, 5

SITUATION

I'm having one of my very low energy days. I feel discouraged, ineffective and defeated. I have a headache.

BODY CUES

Mainly the headache, discouragement and lethargy.

DRILL: Grounding

WHAT HAPPENED

The Grounding drill helped me collect myself. I only did it as an act of obedience. I'm not sure why God has given me this solemn assignment. It makes me feel silly to keep doing these drills, especially the Grounding drill. That one really humbles me.

But the drill helped a lot and I easily sensed the presence of Jesus after I finished walking around – gawky and bird-like – for the "Move" portion.

I sensed quiet comfort from Jesus right here with me. "I'm here. I'm here. All is well." God doesn't look down on me when these low energy days come. The discouragement has shifted into peace knowing that God loves me. I got the idea to pull out my cross-stitch and use this downtime productively so took some Tylenol® and enjoyed the afternoon.

INSIGHT

I've come to realize that doing these drills, as foolish as they seem, is mainly an act of obedience. They have no intrinsic value and it would be a mistake on my part to shoehorn them into anyone else's worship or prayer life. "Hey, if you want to be a super Christian, you really should be doing Stand-Down and Grounding drills."

No. It's more like God asking Ezekiel to sleep on his left side for 390 nights and then on his right side for 40 (Ezekiel 4:1-8). Or it's like Jeremiah and his ever-more-icky "belt" (Jer. 13:1-11). Doing drills this year feels like practice pages of multiplication problems that I do just because my teacher has assigned them. Thinking of it that way, I'm just relieved He's not asking me to do something gross or difficult.

So I bless these silly little drills and ask God to teach me this year whatever He has in mind through the foolishness of gawky bird steps.

Feb. 20: Freeze Mode...And Psalm 131

...I am like a weaned child with its mother;
like a weaned child I am content. Psalm 131:2

SITUATION

During times when I felt sick or on days when I crashed after hard work, why did I hesitate to go pray about it? This troubled me so I finally went to the Lord to hash it out with Him. This entry summarizes the parts for public consumption of that prayer time.

BODY CUES

Definitely on the "Freeze Mode" side of the spectrum. On top of normal fatigue and illness, I also feel resistance, the thought that prayer is hard work and a mental claustrophobia if I get too close to God on days when I'm not at my best.

DRILL

Instead of doing the Grounding drill, which today's cues called for, I pressed in to pray and ask Him for clarification.

WHAT HAPPENED

Looking for a root cause took me to memories of my childhood, roaming the hills behind our house and feeling comforted by the solitude because the dysfunction at home felt claustrophobic. My mother had no friends her own age and poured all her longing for friendship into having me as her best friend. She craved intense, deeply self-disclosing conversations with me but she was not a safe person for me to let down my guard around.

I carried the burden of all her most intense angst on every topic and sometimes I felt the urge to evade her because I couldn't handle it. I was only a child, as young as ten years old, trying to figure out how to comfort and support her in all her adult problems.

She expected me to reciprocate by revealing the intensity of all my teenage angst. She took pleasure in knowing far more than I felt comfortable sharing. At the time it felt wonderful to enjoy such an intense relationship and gave me a hunger for deep friendships. But the built-in dysfunction also tripped me up when I grew into adulthood.

INSIGHTS

I owned up to this history before the Lord and asked Him for help. The phrase from David's prayer in Psalm 131 came to mind, the one about being a weaned child. Quietly some insights came to mind.

"You are afraid I will always demand of you to be intense and intensely engaged to pray. David shows the way. It's OK to be the weaned child on those days when you're weary and spent."

I thought about Psalm 131 and went to look it up.

I see that, unlike my mom, God realizes that some days I can go toe to toe with Him. On those days I'm able to come before Him as a capable, mature, believing adult bringing all my intensity.

He also knows that on other days I'm the fragile child who can't face anyone else's intensity, or even my own usual level of intensity. Those days I just need a safe, friendly landing place for wordless comfort.

Psalm 131 is a great psalm to sit in when we get weary and overwhelmed. It's a great resource, either as an alternative to Grounding Drill or in coordination with it.

I shared the insights about this Psalm with the ladies at the Bible study and they liked adding it to the tool kit for this year's experiments.

Fig. 16 PSALM 131 GROUNDING EXERCISE

The words of Psalm 131	Applying it to Help Us Get Grounded
My heart is not proud, O Lord, my eyes are not haughty;	Come humbly like a child.
I do not concern myself with great matters or things too wonderful for me	Set aside worries and burdens. You don't have to be adult or intense now. You can be a kid.
But I have calmed and quieted myself	Collect yourself using the Grounding drill if you like or just by quieting yourself in whatever way makes sense in the moment.
I am like a weaned child with its mother; like a weaned child I am content.	Relax into His presence in the posture of a yielded, relaxed child. Expect Him to give you mainly wordless comfort or simple reassurance.
Israel, put your hope in the Lord both now and forevermore.	By the end of this quiet time, you will return to a collected frame of mind. You will be able to recall Bible promises and your faith in Jesus. In a comforting tone of voice, "preach the gospel" to your soul, just like David does in this verse. Keep it simple, not complicated.

FEB. 24: FLIGHT MODE...AND DEEP CALLING TO DEEP

SITUATION

I had the privilege of sitting with a dear friend of mine to do healing prayer with her. What she heard when she went to Jesus resonated deeply with my own identity, especially as a follow-up to my last log entry.

(I used to shy away from applying to myself what He says to a healing prayer client but He has encouraged me to enjoy and be blessed by healing truth that resonates for my story as well. He enjoys multitasking. There's plenty of blessing to go around. This session ministered blessing to both of us.)

BODY CUES

Intensity of heart that can be mistaken for Flight Mode but which arises every bit as strongly as an adrenaline rush in the presence of a kindred spirit.

WHAT HAPPENED

The child of brokenness wanders from place to place and has no roots. She develops this intensity of longing to be seen and known. She feels profound disappointment with friends who stay shallow like the seagulls that squabble and bicker and fight over scraps at the beach.

Her brokenness makes her feel like she is always on the outside looking in on the circle of "normal" people. Their intricate rituals and stupid games make no sense to her. The level of their day-to-day struggles seems so elementary compared with the level of difficulty of her trek to wholeness.

It's hard to explain that to seagulls, so why bother?

My friend became silent before the Lord and sensed the Holy Spirit hovering over the face of the deep: hovering and ministering comfort over her uplifted face, then hovering over my uplifted face, then hovering in the *heavenlies* over the invisible face of our Father, searching, knowing, understanding, blessing and appreciating the hidden depths.

She senses a world of difference between the seagulls who gather at the shoreline versus the whales that make their home in the deep. They dive deep into the Word. Their journey to wholeness takes them through deeper pain than others. Their intensity can only be fully expressed in the deep. Whales long for sociable connection with other creatures of the deep and can call to one another from hundreds of miles away. Their pods stay pretty small.

"Deep calls to deep…all Your waves and breakers have crashed over me" (Psalm 42:7).

We bless the Holy Spirit who searches the deep things of God.

APPLICATION FOR MY SITUATION

The session today reminds me that one of the things I most love about God is that He can handle my intensity; so few people can. Weird to say but true. He's not overwhelmed by me or upset when I get intense. He can match it force for force, understand it, know it and know me.

My mom's brokenness left me the legacy of this longing for deep friendship. Even though God's intensity takes some getting used to, I love the intensity of my friendship with God. I don't have to measure my words with Him or worry that He'll dismiss or rebuke where the seagulls in my own world give me blank stares because they just don't get me.

But unlike my mother, God remembers that I'm but dust. He gives me a safe place in which to vent my happy intensity, like this intensity of a short connection with a soul mate, or my intensity to pray or ponder or my intensity of joy when I have a new *Aha! Moment.*

He has been teaching me the needful lesson my mother omitted by also welcoming me when I'm a child with a child's needs and a child's capacity. He receives with grace my intensity of fear or insecurity or utter exhaustion.

And I sense that this year He is teaching me practical ways to moderate that intensity if it gets out of hand. It's possible to let the peace of Christ rule in my heart when it's caught up with intensity of one kind or another. But there might be a middle ground between the seagulls and the deep dwelling whales that allows for simple friendships as well.

5
D-Day

Suddenly it all makes sense…

Feb. 26: Stand Down...And My Heart Attack

SITUATION

First thing every Monday morning, I've had to take a certain nasty medication. This pill always gave me trouble. I stayed close to the bathroom, just in case, and suffered through queasy stomach and general yuckiness until things settled down by around noon. The pill was so caustic to the body that it came with the warning not to lie down for the first thirty minutes.

So, there we were in our jammies, Jim and I, waiting out the half hour until we could sort of enjoy the rest of Jim's day off. Sixteen minutes in, I suddenly felt radiating pain generalized across my whole upper back, pain in my throat and especially up into my mouth. Clearly, something had gone very wrong. We threw on some street clothes and jumped in the car headed for Mt. Zion Hospital.

Jim waited on hold at the Kaiser Help line, and by the time the advice nurse came on the line we were already well on the way. As soon as I described my symptoms she told us, "Pull off the freeway and call 9-1-1."

So we did.

It felt awkward parked by the side of the road just off Imperial Highway. In a few minutes, we heard the siren as the EMTs pulled up behind us. The paramedics helped me climb into the ambulance and, as I lay there on the gurney, my torso suddenly flooded with major tingling, across my whole back, my arms, my throat and mouth. I recognized it as a huge download of adrenaline.

BODY CUES

A lot of radiating pain in my back, throat and mouth, and that sudden massive jolt of adrenaline. Major tension, especially in my arms and jaw.

DRILL: Stand-Down

WHAT HAPPENED

The instant I realized that my body had fired this latest blast of adrenaline, I had two major thoughts that came as blocks of insight, not linear ideas one after another.

First one: "Oh! You knew this day would come! That's why I sensed such urgency in Your voice when You told me to practice, practice, practice these drills!" This gave me immediate and abundant peace of mind that this wasn't unknown to God. Jesus was right here with me in this fancy van. Today's crisis formed part of His plan for me, and He had made sure I would be absolutely ready.

In the second block of thought, my training kicked in and Pilot instantly assessed that it would freak me out if I paid even a moment's attention to the tingling. I completely ignored it and collected myself to deal with this emergency in a calm, assessing, curious and kind sort of way. I focused like a laser – like my life depended on it – on each part of each deep breath and on the rhythm of clenching and unclenching arms and legs. I calmly answered the questions put to me by the paramedic.

INSIGHTS AND OBSERVATIONS

Doing the drills kept me calm that whole first day of my hospital stay. My heart attack stayed extremely mild and I'm convinced that – in my case, not necessarily anyone else's – my training kept me from freaking out which might have worsened the attack.

Throughout that entire stay I alternated between Stand-Down and Grounding drills. Repeatedly assessing and doing the drills kept me steady and in control. It gave my mind something practical to do when all the *What Ifs?* in the world crowded in for attention.

In retrospect, I noticed that my Pilot seemed to instinctively recognize that it was unrealistic to aim for complete calm that day. I was experiencing a major crisis. My mind stayed quite revved up all day. But **Pilot regularly assessed when I began to slip into an extreme of shut down mode or an excessive revving. It aimed to compensate for any imbalance, not completely neutralize it.**

By ignoring the symptoms of that huge adrenaline surge in the ambulance, which would have totally freaked me out, and instead, focusing like a laser on proactively doing the drill, my fear became manageable. On a crisis day when I most needed to keep my wits about me, the goofy little drills had made it possible to do just that.

By the way, that was the last Monday I took that nasty pill.

Feb. 26: Grounding…And Micro-movements

SITUATION

After I got checked in at the emergency room, the ER doctor ordered some tests. All morning long I got wheeled around on my gurney from one test to another. It brought back many unpleasant memories of the last time I had suffered a catastrophic health crisis when I almost died in 2006 in this very same hospital. There's something about getting wheeled around on the gurney, dressed only in the hospital gown and covered by the rumpled white hospital sheet/blankets that quickly reduces a person to a mindset of total helplessness.

The techies steer your gurney through long halls and up or down in the elevator. Usually they drop you off in a hallway and leave you there. It feels like you've been discarded and no one cares. Or they might wheel you all the way into an unfamiliar room and hand you off to other strangers who move you this way and that around scary looking diagnostic machinery.

Either way, just the fact of eventually entering a new room lying on your back, not standing up, puts you at a disadvantage and amps up that helpless feeling. It's nearly impossible to have an adult conversation between equals when most of the people stand over you while you lay there in your jammies as if you were a little girl on a sleepover.

That body posture has already translated in your mind to helplessness before you even begin to factor in the overwhelming sense of helplessness you feel because you have no control over what's going on in your body. Trust me, if you're facing a major health crisis while lying on a gurney, you're talking serious, serious danger. Even people who rarely venture into Freeze Mode in normal life can find this body posture sucking them inexorably into some degree of fearful shut down.

BODY CUES

The main cue, besides whatever physical discomfort, is the experience of getting wheeled around on the gurney and feeling helpless.

DRILL: Grounding

WHAT HAPPENED

I can't express how well the Grounding drill came to my rescue to counteract that vulnerable posture. If only I had known it the last time around! For the first test, the transport assistant wheeled me to an empty hallway outside the CAT scan room and left me there. It was the first time I had been alone that morning. I felt helplessness but remembered my training.

I recalled a story told by Peter A. Levine, one of the pioneering brain researchers who discovered how to help people pull out of Freeze Mode. The secret of the MOVE step in the Grounding drill is that it teaches the terrified Body Brain how to move again. When a person can't move at all, or can't – or shouldn't – get up off the gurney, for instance, grounding reminds the Body Brain that even though we can't move right now, our body still has the capacity to move and will be able to move in a little while. We do this by ***micro-movements.***

Micro-movements: Doing a tiny portion of the drill while we remember the meaning of the full movement.

After years of studying Freeze Mode and micro-movements, one day Peter Levine got hit by a car, and tells the story of putting into practice what he had discovered only in theory.

Lying on the gurney in the ambulance, he wriggled his toes which reassured him that he'd be able to walk again. He also focused on listening to his body. What had his body tried to do to ward off the car? He realized that his hand still felt this urgency to reach out with splayed fingers and block the car from hitting him. So in the ambulance, he flexed his hand as much as possible under the blanket, allowing his hand to sense that it would be able to move to protect him the next time around.

After a gazelle races like crazy to escape the lion, if she outruns it and can safely come to a halt, her whole body will shake violently for a minute or so. Then she'll flick her tail and trot back to the herd as if nothing had happened. Like that gazelle, Levine allowed himself to shiver when the urge came in the ambulance. He knew from his research, that doing the micro-movements and allowing his body to shake off the extra adrenaline meant that he had greatly diminished the odds of getting PTSD symptoms after his accident.

Lying on my gurney in the hallway, I remembered Levine's story. I couldn't do the full FEET part of grounding but I could lie there, access my Pilot, and focus my full attention down to the toes I couldn't see under the blanket. Then I wriggled my toes. I focused on the way the sheets and the chilly hallway felt to my toes. It shifted my mind from feeling scared and helpless to remembering that my toes will be able to move again, Lord willing. Plus it connected my Smart Brain to my Body Brain.

I couldn't do a full drill but did whatever smaller version of centering and labeling I could do while lying on the gurney. I couldn't do the full MOVE part of tensing feet and calf muscles and then getting up to walk my goofy Big Bird steps around my bedroom. But as I wriggled my toes and tensed one leg and then the other I pictured the toes remembering their muscles and walking again.

After a few minutes of grounding and collecting myself, I felt calm enough to sense Jesus right there with me in the hallway. My heart overflowed with gratitude that He had prepared me for this day.

I sensed His quiet voice reassuring me, "Dionne, be at peace. This is not your time. You are NOT going to die today."

The words of my theme verse ran through my mind, "Let the peace of Christ rule in your heart …" (Wait a minute...**heart**? **HEART!**)…" and I laughed out loud.

"Oh! My **heart!** Now that's hilarious!"

I was still chuckling when the door opened and the lab assistant wheeled my gurney into the lab.

6
Upping the Ante

This adventure showed that
I have a lot more work to do

Feb. 27: Flight Mode…And the Challenge to Up the Ante

I sought the Lord and He answered me;
He delivered me from all my fears. Psalm 34:4

SITUATION

I didn't sleep all night at the hospital. The heart doctor insisted on complete bed rest until the angiogram next morning which would assess the damage. I used the drills all night to stay calm. The happy calm of daytime hours turned into grim battle. One after another after another, the *What Ifs?* crowded in upon me – fears about my health or my future or my death and on and on.

Each nightmare wave of terror painted its dread scenario of vivid inevitability. But after each wave of fear I chose to shift into bare-knuckled trust. I couldn't control my mind going a million miles an hour. But, God helping me all that awful night, I would eventually wrestle control over the direction of my thoughts. For some reason I never did win once-and-for-all peace that night but, time and again, I gutted it out until I could surrender each fear to God's sovereign will.

If I have to endure this scenario I will trust You for it. That possibility scares me to death, but if I have to go through that, I know You'll give me strength to bear it.

DRILL: Both drills, repeatedly

WHAT HAPPENED

The nurses told Jim how much time to expect the test to take. If they needed to put in a stent they would do it on the spot and if they decided I needed heart surgery they would scope out their plan of action, close me up and schedule it as soon as possible.

A quick thirty minutes later, they came out all smiles. They found no damage to the heart, no blockages or plaque buildup. They just found a tear on one of the coronary arteries and their experience had taught them to leave those little rips alone to heal naturally. My heart attack had been caused by a SCAD event – a Spontaneous Coronary Artery Dissection.

It was a huge answer to prayer! Within an hour we were back in our car heading home.

INSIGHTS AND TAKE AWAYS

That night in the hospital marked a milestone in my walk with the Lord. It took me back to the season, eight years before, when I had tackled one particular besetting fear (my fears about finances), not one episode at a time, but as a whole and asked God to deliver me from that fear once and for all. He did so and that particular fear lost much of its grip on me.

I see that in this season of post-Medicare eligibility, the central battle for people my age is the battle against fear. Fear in all its forms, fear that inexorably pushes in on us to draw the circle of what we do and what we're brave enough to attempt smaller and smaller until we find our circle so small we're stuck in a bed and die.

So this ups the ante for this year of experiments. This crisis turned into a pop quiz of what I fear and which fears I need to actively address so I'll face the next hospital night – God forbid! – with a more robust and operational peace of Christ at work to combat runaway fears.

I've been given a new Job #1 this year: Learn how to master fear so that the peace of Christ actually rules in my heart no matter the crisis. It makes total sense to focus like a laser on Colossians 3:15 this year and do these silly little drills. The stakes are higher than I thought. I can shudder my way through the days left of my life, beset by fears and at the mercy of any *What Ifs?* that pop into my head. Or I can accept God's kind invitation to cultivate Pilot, up the ante and learn how to live in the felt security of the peace of Christ.

I couldn't pull it off last night in the hospital to rest – really rest – guarded by His peace. But if there's a next time, teach me how to do better. I want to be like Caleb in the Bible who volunteered to tackle the biggest giant when he was eighty-five. Years ago, God pointed out some verses and said, "This is you." In them He promised I will bear fruit in old age. Might be nice to actually believe that.

I accept Your challenge.

My Life Verses
Psalm 92:12-15

The righteous will flourish like a palm tree,
they will grow like a cedar of Lebanon,
Planted in the house of the Lord,
they will flourish in the courts of our God.
They will still bear fruit in old age,
they will stay fresh and green,
Proclaiming, "The Lord is upright; He is my Rock,
and there is no wickedness in Him."

Feb. 28: Flight Mode...And the Leaven of the Pharisees

SITUATION

For the first time since we bought our Corolla two years ago, I didn't earn enough by paid counseling appointments to at least cover the full car payment plus over and above for tax and tithe. It had already been a slower month than usual and then the heart attack bumped the last three appointments into next month.

DRILL: Stand-Down

WHAT HAPPENED

The realization of the shortfall had thudded into my mind this morning. Time stood still for me while I weighed my response. A half-formed worry hovered at the fringes of my mind ready to leap into action. And into that pause, I invited the God of Peace to show me how to up the ante.

"Watch out! Beware of the leaven of the Pharisees!"

The phrasing came from all my years using the New American Standard of the Bible. It was as if I heard Jesus boom that warning to his disciples who had forgotten to bring bread.

Oh! He's talking to me. I grabbed my Bible and looked it up. Jesus spoke this same warning regarding two types of unbelief: the unbelief that refuses to admit when God has done a miracle, and the unbelief that questions whether God will provide. I felt conviction for the second kind of unbelief.

Mark 8:14-21 (especially verses 17-21) spoke to my situation.

"'Why do you discuss the fact that you have no bread? Are your hearts hardened? Do you not yet see or understand?...And do you not remember, when I broke the five loaves for the five thousand, how many baskets full of broken pieces you picked up?'

"They said to Him, 'Twelve.'

"'And when I broke the seven loaves for the four thousand, how many large baskets of broken pieces did you pick up?'

"And they said to Him, 'Seven.'

"And He was saying, 'Do you not yet understand?'"

INSIGHTS

The disciples didn't get it that Jesus had taken full responsibility to provide for every need during the entire time they hung out with Him. Sometimes He provided through the intermediary of generous friends or hospitable strangers or by timely strolls through grain fields. Sometimes He performed a miracle and the disciples also ate their fill of the bread they passed to the crowds.

God has promised complete and daily provision to anyone who asks Him to "give us this day our daily bread." Not ***barely*** enough but ***more than*** enough. He provides and then we figure out what to do with the leftovers.

Notice what He specifically draws to their attention:

- Not the **need** (the hungry crowds or the hungry disciples).
- Not even the **massive provision** (bread enough to feed thousands on more than one occasion).
- But the baskets heaped full of **leftovers!**

He urges them to keep their eyes on the leftovers AFTER the miracle. We express our faith by remembering the **overabundance** of His supply. Yes, He provided enough for 5000 men and their families. But after every person had eaten their fill **and were satisfied**, they had ample bread left over.

In Jordan Peterson's bestseller, *12 Rules for Life*, he makes the comment that our external environment gives us way too many pieces of visual input, which makes it impossible to grasp it all. Because the human eye can't process all of it, it relies on the brain to prioritize where to focus the attention.

"You see what you look at." (For a fun illustration, Peterson suggests you run a search on YouTube® for "The Monkey Business Illusion.")

Jesus tells us to keep our eyes fixed on the leftovers, and that it expresses faith in Him when we decide to look at leftovers instead of today's forgotten bread or yesterday's miracle.

ONE ADDITIONAL COMMENT

I'm endlessly touched by the kindness of Jesus. I struggled with fears about finances partly because my capacity to trust anyone had been broken by the abuse I suffered. He understood why I struggled with those fears so long.

He could have "dumped the truck" on me early on by jumping to today's insight back at the beginning. If He had started with this challenging and somewhat daunting message, it would have shamed and discouraged my tiny faith, and I would have given up long ago. Back then there wasn't a chance in a million that I could have pulled it off to erase any last trace of the yeast of unbelief.

Instead, He won my trust like a kindhearted person winning the trust of a bedraggled little feral cat. I always found the milk waiting for me on the porch. For one crisis after another He provided what we needed, and allowed me to notice His relentless faithfulness afterwards. He patiently built a track record of provision that nurtured my wobbly trust.

He provided even when I flat didn't believe. He taught me about "Manna Time" (which I'll discuss in more detail a few pages from now). He was the One who encouraged me to start keeping a journal of any financial need that caused me even a flicker of worry. Now, years later, that journal overflows with evidence. He's the One who has answered EVERY single request and met EVERY single need.

It wasn't until today that I heard that stern tone from Him to rid myself of unbelief and rest in His provision. Knock it off! Believe and be done with it! Even a pinch of unbelief will contaminate the whole loaf.

Ok. It's about time. I'm ready.

P.S. I laughed out loud when, a few days before the March car payment came due, we got two refund checks in the mail out of the blue that exactly covered the shortfall. To the penny!

March 6: Stand Down...And La Maze® Training

SITUATION

The first Tuesday back at the *Trust Training* Bible study, we did a little show-and-tell of how the drills had worked for me during my little SCAD adventure and how others were practicing the drills and getting good results.

INSIGHTS

Two cool comments to share.

First, when I sensed God give the assignment to do these drills this year, that task exemplifies *Trust Training* at its best. In Chapter One of that Bible study, we define Trust Training this way:

TRUST TRAINING
Viewing all my problems and difficult circumstances through two dimensions:

1. As a particular problem to be solved or handled, and
2. As a training exercise, wisely given by God to help me learn how to trust Him

We focus on a specific little training exercise tailored to hone the practical skill of trusting God for today's *crisis du jour* or this season's unique challenges. We ask God to teach us how to trust Him and then practice trusting Him in that simple way.

Even though I teach this stuff all the time, somehow it escaped my notice that God had given me a perfect trust training exercise in the Stand Down and Grounding drills. That training kicked in when my world shook in the ambulance on the way to Mt. Zion Hospital. Doing the drills had increased my practical ability to trust in God during an adrenaline crisis.

Second, an *Aha! Moment*! These drills are a La Maze exercise for fear! Back in the day when I was a young mom, most pregnant women would learn the La Maze method. We trained for birth and delivery using specific breathing exercises, and trained ourselves to fiercely focus on an object when the pain got severe.

Sound familiar?

La Maze helped me tremendously in the delivery of both my sons. It kept me in control at what is typically the most out of control experience of a young woman's life. The breathing exercises seemed goofy and awkward when Jim and I sat cross-legged on the floor at La Maze classes. But they suddenly made perfect sense during labor and delivery. The gangly efforts in class practicing with Jim, my newbie La Maze coach, trained him to act the role of knowledgeable, empathetic Pilot to calmly help me through the ordeal.

Stand Down functions just like La Maze and so does Grounding. And we can practice it for any fear, not just when the contractions hit.

Who knew?

March 8: Fight Mode...And the Quicker Cutoff

SITUATION

Yesterday I heard about a former friend's latest shocking antic and it made me furious – not fretting level of anger, or irritation level of anger but hair-on-fire level of rage. This latest behavior scandalized me and the sheer ingratitude of the stunt took my breath away. I wanted to jump in the car and go yell and scream. I hesitate to admit this but the best words that captured what I felt were all profanities I wouldn't ever say in normal life.

Naturally I did all this ranting in the privacy of my own house. Now I wouldn't have actually gone over to yell my curse words in person. And I knew it would be unwise in the extreme to talk to any of my friends while in that frame of mind. Jim did his best to calm me down and that helped a lot but soon something else would come to my mind and I'd be off and running on a new rant.

BODY CUES

Whole body revved to the max, clenched muscles especially in my face and arms, all my thoughts consumed by anger, outrage and a fierce sense of injustice.

DRILL:

I had the ability to step back into Pilot and could tell I needed to do Stand-Down but I didn't because I couldn't yet. I did go pray about it after I had calmed down enough.

WHAT HAPPENED & WHAT I LEARNED

The instructions I got on New Year's Day came to my rescue: "Whatever comes up, start looking for guidance at Col. 3:15 and then widen the circle to the rest of Colossians 3." It was glaringly obvious that Jesus and I were going to have a little heart to heart chat about verse 8 and I would calm down by looking up some Greek vocabulary.

Col. 3:8 with the defined word in bold	Meaning of the Greek
*"But **now***	this present moment, immediately
*you must **rid yourself** of all such things as these:*	put away, cast off, discard
anger,	(Greek word is orge); passion, indignation
rage,	passion as if breathing hard
malice,	badness, depravity, malignity, evil or trouble
***slander,** and*	blasphemy, vilification, especially against God, evil speaking, railing
***filthy language** from your lips."*	vile conversation, gutter talk, curse words

I see no wiggle room. This ups the ante big-time. What do I do with this?

In my spirit, a phrase from Psalm 37:8, about fretting, came to mind and I heard this thought: **"You are fretting because of an evil doer. Yes, [this person] has done what you accuse. But I'm looking at you, Didi. I call you to peace."**

I confessed my own sins of anger, rage, slander and cursing. I chose to forgive this person and the pain they have caused.

Now much calmer, I asked more about the clear sense I had that He is upping the ante on what He will allow without rebuke. I have been operating by the guideline of Eph. 4:26, 27.

> In your anger do not sin. Do not let the sun go down on your anger.
> Do not give the devil a foothold.

I thought I had leeway to vent for a few hours. This feels like a big shift for my story. Back when I was a child and got angry at the abuse, I could never get it cleared out by sundown. Day after day I endured one outrage after another with no mechanism for resolution except to stuff my anger and hunker down to get through one more day.

Like most dysfunctional homes, my brothers and I were trained not to feel. The unspoken message went something like this: "As the adults we will do anything we jolly well feel like doing to you. We will betray your trust over and over, we will punish you at unpredictable times for no particular reason, we will violate your innocence, we will scare the wits out of you, and your job is to just take it. And shut up. And not even register your fear or pain by the least flicker of a glance or the whimper of a smothered cry."

Anger was not allowed in any form in us children. Parents could scream and yell and betray and hit. We were not allowed to react.

One of the first hurdles of the newbie to counseling is that terrifying prospect of saying anything about how we feel. It's a positive sign when we finally realize that it's ok now to voice all those stifled words or stuffed feelings.

Unfortunately, once we sense permission to speak freely, out gushes this avalanche of anger that had no opportunity for closure before. In fact, my main visual of my entire journey to wholeness pictures me with a little bucket, slowly emptying a seemingly bottomless abyss of anger.

In kindness, although I felt horribly guilty and ashamed that I held so much anger, I never once felt God's condemnation while I methodically shoveled anger out, one bucketful at a time, processed it, forgave that bit, and reached down to scoop out the next batch. It took upwards of two decades to drain that abyss of anger until I finally sensed a serene inward lake of crystal clear water where that anger had roiled around for so long.

Like so many other abuse victims who become competent to function in adult life, I learned how to control anger in my day to day life. The dysfunctional training comes in handy to stuff anger on the job or with your annoying neighbor. Jim taught me how to parent our sons in a healthier, non-angry way. And I'm grateful that being a pastor's wife kept me between the guardrails by motivating me to stifle the ungodly urge to lash out at people.

It pleased God a lot that I worked so hard to drain my abyss. It would have been nice to drain it all in one big cathartic weekend. But doing the work, year after year, one slimy bucketful at a time, obeyed this verse because I tackled it *now*. I see miserable ladies in their sixties who went through my kind of abuse still lugging around their topped off anger abyss. They didn't tackle it *now*, back when they sensed the prompting to go fix it *now* when they were in their thirties. They let their grievances and anger burble on and on and on, metastasizing into deeper poison.

A NEW SET OF MARCHING ORDERS

But what does it look like now, after I've drained my own abyss? After I've learned how to set aside the anger that covers my more vulnerable feelings? After You've spent the last several years teaching me how to become a woman of peace? How do You want me to up the ante when it comes to dealing with anger?

Martin Luther talked about those precious times when the Holy Spirit begins to preach to our spirit. That began to happen to me. Suddenly in quick succession, my mind recalled specific verses with a brief insight and reminder for each one as if He flipped the pages and pointed out the words.

Ephesians 4:26, 27 was our first stop. "Do not let the sun go down on your anger" gives a very specific deadline. Hey, feel free to knock yourself out getting really angry for a short while (but don't sin, which I had done this day). You can think it out and voice what would be healthy to voice. But let it go by bedtime.

As much as I had flipped, as angry as I had gotten, I was perfectly capable of dealing with that anger. I got the sense that, **"You have no leftover anger from childhood to hold you back. Time is officially up on that get-out-of-jail-free card that exempted you from obeying that entire command as written. Let your anger go by nightfall. No excuses. Start now."**

We quickly turned to Psalm 37:8, 9:

> **Refrain** from anger and **turn away** from wrath;
> **do not** fret, it leads only to evil.
> For those who are evil will be destroyed
> but those who hope in the Lord will inherit the land.

Notice that this raises the bar yet again. Refrain from anger. Don't even give it permission. This doesn't piggyback on the dysfunctional message of the abuser who doesn't allow us to have a voice. My wise Savior had given me full permission and had strengthened my hand to drain my abyss. I have found my voice. I can choose to voice anger or I can choose to refrain from anger as an act of my will. And He pointed out that now I need to start choosing to refrain from full-throated rage.

I'm doing these experiments this year on flight, fight or freeze. **But it's time to put into mothballs the upper end of my own Fight Mode. Let this day be the last day of that degree of anger. Let this be a memo to Pilot to shut it down before it gets that far out of hand.**

I accepted this instruction with no hesitation. The love of my Jesus surrounded me with such kindness and gave me so much encouragement that this was something I could do now. In that sweetness, my heart sensed His comfort to me about that situation that so angered me today. I sensed that I could be at peace. God had that situation well in hand. His attention was on me.

"This is the time for you to make a major shift forward into strict self-control. I've called you to be a woman of peace. You're ready for this next phase. So allow no room for rage. No room for filthy talk. You have a blessing to give. Your mouth must remain clean to speak My healing words."

At the end I sensed His agreement that the person's action had shown ingratitude and that it rightly warrants great indignation. But don't point fingers. "Take that to heart to live in *eucharisteo* yourself [intentional, whole-hearted gratitude]."

"Let the peace of Christ rule in **your** heart…"

March 16: Stand Down...And Sharon's Story

I am a teacher of 24 eight-year-olds. Sometimes when I see frustration levels rising I try the Stand-Down drill.

A couple of months ago I practiced with my class. We came up to the carpet. I turned off the lights. We took our shoes off, rubbed our feet, and put on new socks. We took 4-5 slow deep breaths, focusing on being calm. We rolled our muscles out, relaxing the tension in our arms, legs, and neck.

While students were breathing and relaxing muscles, I used calming words like "It's okay." "Relax." "Breathe." I also like to add soft music for a more serene atmosphere.

You can see the difference in children even after just a few minutes. They need to recognize their feelings and learn how to calm down.

Mar. 18: Flight Mode...And Manna Time

SITUATION

In the aftermath of hearing the command to "Beware of the Leaven of the Pharisees" as it related to my fears about financial concerns, I've been enjoying the opportunity to refresh my memory about "Manna Time," a phrase I mentioned in that log entry but didn't explain.

I learned many of the basic principles that became "Manna Time" back when Jim and I did church-planting. But financial fears had been a topic I had wrestled with for most of my life. It came to a head in 2010 and I went to God and asked Him to deliver me from my fears about finances, not just episode by episode, but once and for all.

I did a huge crash course on this topic to get a handle on the financial fears that still remained. For about ten weeks I studied the Scriptures intensely, focusing on times God provided in a lavish, supernatural way. What could I learn from the story of manna in the wilderness, Elijah during the drought, and Jesus feeding the 5000 and the 4000?

Instead of writing a new explanation, I've included an excerpt from a devotional I wrote up a few years ago for the devotional book Jim and I did together.

A DEFINITION OF "MANNA TIME"

…thin flakes like frost on the ground appeared on the desert floor. When the Israelites saw it, they said to each other, "What is it?" For they did not know what it was.
Exodus 16:14b, 15

My husband and I have been in ministry for thirty-three years. Church planting frequently takes planters to the razor edge of financial uncertainty. Often we didn't know at the first of the month how we'd pay bills due in that month.

At first this used to scare the wits out of me. However, as time passed, I began to realize that we were always held safely within two alternating types of time that I eventually dubbed "Regular Time" and "Manna Time." During *Regular Time* God provides for His own through normal, predictable streams of income like jobs, regular paychecks, financial supporters, investments, inheritance or whatever. During *Regular Time*, God provides for us indirectly, using ordinary economic channels available to everyone – believers and unbelievers alike.

During *Manna Time*, those normal, predictable streams of income dry up, at least temporarily. Supporters don't send what they promised, side jobs end, or the bills far outweigh our resources to pay them. During *Manna Time,* God provides for us directly, using non-traditional methods like serendipities, so-called coincidences, the divinely compelled kindness of others and outright miracles.

Jim and I emphatically testify that God ALWAYS provided what we absolutely needed. It took me a long while to recognize when God had switched us into *Manna Time*, longer still to learn the precious lessons of manna….

Quoted from a devotional of mine in *Daily Encouragement in the Church-Planting Journey: 365 Days of Wisdom, Inspiration, and Courage for Church Planters by Church Planters*
Jim Carpenter Editor

NEW INSIGHTS

I loved the deep dive that taught me so much more about Manna Time. At the end of that ten-week period, I felt prompted to set up a log of financial requests and answers. I included the Bible promises God had quickened to my heart and the personal encouragements I had heard during the long seasons of prayer.

For the past eight years, any time a financial concern rises to the level of causing even a flutter of anxiety, I get out my log and write out the specifics of the request in black ink, including the date and the dollar amount. When God answers the request and provides what we need, I go back and record the date and dollar amount using red ink. At this moment, I have NO old requests for which God didn't provide. I have a few current items but they are well within the time frame of how quickly God tends to provide.

It's been so cool to read through those entries. God has been incredibly faithful. It was cool to see that God used that log as training wheels of sorts to help me deal with financial concerns in a constructive, faith-filled way. I have taken this most recent Leaven-of-the-Pharisees word as an encouragement to let go of even that first flutter of anxiety.

Even before the challenge last month, I had noticed that lately I pull out the journal less often for even large financial needs. The weight of evidence of red-filled pages has calmed most impulses to worry when the new *crisis du jour* comes up.

I don't write poetry ordinarily but by the time I concluded that Manna Time study, a new song arose in my heart that captured my relief and gratitude. I designed a cross-stitch wall hanging and stitched upwards of a dozen of them using that tactile project to embed the truths of it into my bones. What a blessing to notice once again the one I kept that hangs in our kitchen while God encourages me to up the ante.

MANNA TIME

Angels guard this place,
Manna always falls on time,
The jug of oil never runs dry,
And songbirds drop bread at our door.
Hallelujah!

7
A Season of Feeling Yucky

Some low days and various challenges provide good opportunities to use the drills and discover truths only learned in weakness

March 26: The Peace of Christ...And the Blessing of Benjamin

SITUATION

The other night a flare up of my heart symptoms was so severe I took a Nitro pill. So today when I went to the follow-up appointment with my cardiologist, he decided to keep me on my medications longer. He added a few new pills and also ordered a number of tests to rule out some troublesome possibilities.

I prayed about it that evening. Not sure how I feel about the whole thing.

How would You like me to approach You as the God of Peace this evening?

Immediately I thought of the blessing of Benjamin that Moses gave near the end of his career. It's a favorite blessing of mine. I rested in a comfortable position, as if God was shielding me this evening.

> Let the beloved of the Lord rest secure in Him for He shields [her] all day long,
> and the one the Lord loves rests between His shoulders. Deut. 33:12

WHAT HAPPENED

"It's going to be all right," I heard in my spirit. The idea came to me that this would be a year of medical stuff coming up but to rest in Him. Consider this verse a promise for this year. My heart episode had brought up several issues that need to be addressed. Take this as the right time to work through them methodically one by one. View this year as an opportunity to tune up for the next season of life, to get squared away on the medical things and learn how to let the peace of Christ rule in a variety of amped up situations.

I felt the assurance that this season won't last forever. Good health will return. "Allow it to unfold in a peaceful way."

March 30: Stand Down...And Wooziness

BODY CUES

Constant headache and wooziness caused by the new meds. Feeling a little disoriented after scheduling the three MRIs, the biopsy, the cardio appointments and the sleep study to see whether I have sleep apnea. Feeling pretty yucky.

DRILL: Stand-Down

WHAT HAPPENED

Stand-Down helped me collect myself. I heard the gentle reminder, "Beware the Leaven of the Pharisees," which helped me to trust Him for these practical needs.

The passage from Philippians 4:12b, 13 came to mind.

> I have learned the secret of being content in any and every situation,
> whether well-fed or hungry, whether living in plenty or in want.
> I can do all this through Him who gives me strength.

I prayed for my headache and wooziness.

Please heal me if it pleases You. If not, I am content to go through discomfort, thanking You for giving me strength.

April 4: Grounding…And Rediscovering Agency

SITUATION

This morning I woke up tired and listless, finding it hard to get moving. It felt good to do Grounding and to conclude the time rejoicing that "By my God I can scale a wall."

I meditated on that feeling of empowerment. It reminded me of a recent session with a client going through a horrendous ordeal these days who wakes up each morning with her stomach tied up in knots of panic. She felt pretty uptight at the beginning of our session and found it hard to hear from Jesus directly. So I asked her to check in with her stomach.

What did it need for her to do?

Instinctively her hands, one on top of the other, covered her stomach. The fingers splayed wide to double-cover the most territory in a protective and motherly posture. The warmth and kindness from her hands relaxed the tension and calmed her fear.

We noted that her hands had power to calm her stomach. Later on in the session, during a time of quietness, she had no difficulty connecting with Jesus.

DRILL: A modified Grounding

INSIGHT

I've noticed when people do the Grounding drill it does more than help us find Jesus, much as we aim always to end up in His presence. When we're agitated or discouraged, it's just as important to rediscover our own capacity to act. The fancy term for that is ***agency***.

> **Agency** is the capacity to act,
> to do things independently of others,
> to act on our own behalf as a free agent.

When I asked my client what her stomach needed and she moved her hands in a specific meaningful gesture, it reawakened her sense of agency and helped her remember that she doesn't need to panic first thing each morning. She has the capacity to act. She's a smart girl and she will make it through this awful time. God's right there with her but she knew that. She had forgotten that she had hands that could act successfully.

The angel of the Lord told Gideon, "Go in the strength you have" (Judges 6:14).

That's agency.

In these drills we activate both parts: sensing "God with us here" as He promised, ready to help us out, and remembering our own capacity to act, to master our racing thoughts or to calm our fearful, overwhelmed heart.

Paul speaks to both parts in Phil. 4:13.

- My agency: "I can do all things…"
- God's part: "…through Him who gives me strength."

And we see it in our go-to verse in Psalm 18:29:

- God's part: "By my God…"
- My agency: "…I can scale a wall."

April 22: Freeze Mode...And Infirmity

SITUATION

Have had two rugged weeks when it was a struggle to maintain the peace of Christ. I've been slogging through the medical procedures, the back to back MRIs and the biopsy. I felt sick. Infirm. It was hard to walk so I bought better walking shoes. The sleep study and the blizzard of medication information and side effects have swamped me.

DRILL: Grounding

WHAT HAPPENED

Afterwards I asked Jesus for help. How can I walk in peace? I looked at II Cor. 12: 9, 10.

> But He said to me, "My grace is sufficient for you, for My power is made perfect in weakness." Therefore I will boast all the more gladly about my weaknesses, so that Christ's power may rest on me. That is why, for Christ's sake, I delight in weaknesses, in insults, in hardships, in persecutions, in difficulties. For when I am weak, then I am strong.

I wondered how Paul would have boasted in the infirmities I'm dealing with these days.

Lord, I give You these infirmities. Please restore my body and help my legs so I can walk. In the meantime, help me not to get overwhelmed by all this medical stuff. Is there anything You want me to hear that will help Your peace to rule today?

INSIGHTS

I sensed in my spirit a calm reply that communicated the following encouragement and game plan. I got the sense to keep my eyes on Him. He will guide me through this season and it will end well.

But there's no getting around the fact that I am getting older and some of these signs of aging will not go away. To some degree, my body will dictate how much I can do. I will be tempted to withdraw from life and curl in on myself.

As I've mentioned before, older people must battle against fear. That's my battle today. I recognize that often, the reality of our aging bodies can draw our circle smaller without our permission. But I don't want to be like the ones who no longer set new goals here among the living. They let fear shut them down before they actually finish the race God has set before them.

I must resist that urge. Apparently, He has more ministry for me to do. So I can allow Kaiser to help me shift things around to set up good habits to prolong my life.

I embrace that and receive His comfort.

April 24: Stand-Down...And Breath Prayers

SITUATION

In our ongoing *Trust Training* Bible Study group, we just got to Chapter 10 on how to find the safe place to fight the battle. Another Aha! Oh! Both of our drills use breath prayers! They're even geared to operate in synch with our inhale and exhale.

If you haven't read my *Trust Training* book, breath prayers are a great strategy to use when you're hip deep in a crisis and don't have the luxury of taking a break to go pray at length. They're a quick prayer, usually one sentence long or two quick phrases like "Help me, Jesus!" or "Have mercy on me, a sinner!" or "Father, Hide me!"

The ladies and I have found them quite helpful and practical. Breath prayers work great in crisis situations like, well, exactly like when we flip into Survivor Mode. And it's so great. We already know how to do Breath Prayers, and they're easy to teach if people haven't run across them before. Many Christians instinctively pray breath prayers when they're scared to death.

By the way, since I have a hard time walking and chewing gum at the same time, I pray the phrase silently in timing with my inhale and exhale but don't say the words out loud.

BREATH PRAYERS WE ALREADY USE AND HOW TO SAY THEM:

INHALE	EXHALE
"Dear Jesus"	"Help Me now"
"It's OK to stand down"	"All is well."
"I breathe IN Your peace"	"I breathe OUT this stress."
"By my God"	"I can scale a wall."

ADDITIONAL IDEAS

The *Trust Training* book recommends that when we find ourselves locked in a challenging situation, that we figure out an appropriate breath prayer. For instance, if our trust battle includes a money struggle we might craft a breath prayer like "My God will supply / all I need" or "My eyes / are on You." If we're dealing with a health crisis we may use "Be my strength / when I have no strength" or "Be brave! / "It's just a wave!"

As I experiment this spring, it feels most comfortable to use the breath prayers suggested for each drill while I did the actual drill, but then to use breath prayers specific to the current situation after I have collected myself.

Just the other day something reminded me of one of my favorite breath prayers. It's from a meaningful time years ago when I was on the receiving end of healing prayer and I heard, **"The One who loves me is here / so all will be well."** I loved that one so well that I created a cross-stitch wall hanging of those words. It ministers deeply to my spirit. That breath prayer works really well at the ending of a drill and makes it so easy to just shift gears into welcoming the presence of Jesus.

8
A Closer Look at Pilot

Hmm. Maybe there's more to Pilot than I first thought. I wonder...

April 26: Pilot...And Connecting to the Rock

SITUATION

"I'm having trouble connecting to my Pilot. When I notice that I've gotten upset, I pull out my cheat notes and look around for that calm, detached part of my brain observing the rest. But all I can sense is the fogginess and anxiety inside my head. What can I do? How can I find my Pilot?"

My anonymous client (whom I'll call Elaine) had attended my workshop and jumped at the chance to do experiments with me this year. I knew that her childhood had been an absolute nightmare. She still regularly shuts down into Freeze Mode, even as an adult, so we both realized that she came by these Pilot difficulties honestly.

Like other children who shut down often to survive abuse, her barely formed Pilot got turned off repeatedly and hadn't fully developed to her satisfaction. And because this led to such a high degree of anxiety as her normal state, it made total sense that she would find it hard to locate within her mind a part that was calm, assessing, curious and kind.

(By the way, other developmentally challenged children or children on the autism spectrum may also have difficulty developing a functioning Pilot. Also, some people find it difficult to visualize any sort of abstract idea like Pilot. When they close their eyes, all they see is the back of their eyelids.)

Anyway, back to Elaine, she became a Christian in her teens. It saved her life in more ways than one. She grew in her faith by leaps and bounds and the Word of God became precious to her. She had joined a caring church where she got to know supportive friends who encouraged her to go get Christian counseling. By the time I met her, she had become a mature believer who was making solid progress in her journey to wholeness while knowing she had a long distance to go yet.

Elaine and I had an interesting discussion that allowed me an opportunity to think out loud about what I've learned thus far. And as we discussed her situation, we came up with several practical strategies to try out.

Hey, we're already doing experiments anyway, it might be fun to do a few specifically focused on Pilot.

I loved our discussion that day. It encouraged and energized both of us. When I followed up later, Elaine reported that she was having more success finding her Pilot. Some of what I'll share here might have application mainly to her extreme situation. But I'm guessing a lot of us may still feel kind of wobbly about finding that calm, assessing, curious and kind observer when we hunt around for our own Pilot.

WHAT HAPPENED

We discussed three topics:

1. Finding Pilot,
2. Finding the calm, assessing voice in our head, and
3. Finding solid ground to stand on when our brain feels especially foggy.

1. FINDING PILOT

A word of encouragement might be helpful here. We don't have to hunt for Pilot all over the place in our Emotional Brain, Body Brain and the data centers of our Smart Brain. Pilot stays put, so to speak, and already "notices" from its *permanent* position of being detached a bit from the rest of the brain and *above* the rough and tumble of the stirred up emotions, monitoring the entire brain. **Just pay attention to whatever part of your brain it was that spotted something.**

"Look again at what you just said when you described your problem: 'When I ***notice*** I've gotten upset…' That's Pilot! When you notice upset, just latch on to that thought that noted your upset. Make it easy on yourself. If you simply turn your attention to that 'Noticer' thought and follow that thought, it will automatically pull you up alongside it into an observer spot."

2. FINDING THE CALM, ASSESSING VOICE

Elaine was in good company with this dilemma. Many of us have a hard time finding the calm, assessing, curious and kind part of our own mind. Especially if we often struggle with flight, fight or freeze, we likely operate mostly from the exact opposite mental persona. When we get quiet, the first thing that leaps out is the "Angry Dad" voice. Or angry mom. So it's not surprising that we talk to ourselves in a horrible voice that's freaked out, clueless, critical and harsh – even cruel. No wonder it's hard to identify a part of our internal world that speaks or thinks in that calmer voice.

I asked Elaine**, "Can you think of a person in your circle of friends who regularly talks to you in an encouraging tone of voice with words that are calm, assessing, curious and kind?"** Elaine thought of several people right away – teachers, counselors and trusted friends. One friend especially came to mind whose voice brought to mind nothing but encouragement and steady supportiveness.

"I wonder if it would help you find that kindly, calm part of yourself if you thought of your Pilot as having **her** voice." When we kicked around that idea, Elaine realized that she already does hear her friend's calm voice in her head. That friend had already taught her a great deal about how to mentally step back and take stock of a situation. It felt better to assign a familiar voice as her official "Pilot voice," a voice she already knows well and already trusts to calm her down.

If this is a problem for you, Gentle Reader, which voice in your circle of friends might best fit the bill?

3. FINDING SOLID GROUND WHEN OUR BRAIN FEELS FOGGY

I didn't have a clue what to do about this problem so, as I always do in that case, I asked if we could stop and ask God for wisdom using the promise from James 1:5. "If any of you lacks wisdom, you should ask God who gives generously to all without finding fault, and it will be given to you." We both stopped and waited quietly to see what came to mind.

The answer that came to us falls way outside the parameters of the instruction on the YouTube® videos or the Wellness Classes that teach the drills at my health care provider. It reflected the unique two-sided focus this year of learning the mechanics of the drills at the same time we learn how to find the peace of Christ for Flight, Fight and Freeze.

The word "Rock" came to mind in a block of thought that included several related ideas all focused on the verses below, from the end of the Sermon on the Mount (Matthew 7:24, 25).

> Therefore, everyone who hears these words of Mine and puts them into practice is like a wise man who built his house on the rock. The rain came down, the streams rose, and the winds blew and beat against that house; yet it did not fall, because it had its foundation on the rock.

What about applying this idea to Pilot? We reviewed Elaine's story. She heard the gospel and accepted Jesus as her Savior. She embraced Christianity whole-heartedly, studied her Bible and learned how to pray. She goes to church faithfully and serves in various ministries.

According to this promise, for all these years Elaine has been building her house on the rock. Even during all her struggles with Freeze Mode and mental fogginess, she has steadily built a spiritual house with a solid foundation on that rock. That Rock is a safe place to hang out when the storms come.

Fig. 17: FINDING PILOT

We apply that truth in many more ways than just for doing our little drills. But we sensed a kindly invitation to apply it here and now to accessing Pilot. In Fig. 17, "Finding Pilot," our familiar little cartoon makes it look like we step back up into nothingness when we access Pilot. That's not true. Remember we said:

Pilot ≠ Our Christian self,
but when we access Pilot we also access our Christian self.

So let's play with that idea and add a new element in Fig. 18, "Finding the Rock." I encouraged her to practice imagining that when she steps up into Pilot, she doesn't step up into foggy nothingness. She stands atop the solid rock that Jesus promised to us in the Sermon on the Mount.

Fig. 18: FINDING THE ROCK

We step up to the Rock in whatever way makes sense to us. It may help to remember when we became a Christian. Or it may help if we remind ourselves of an important milestone that meant a lot to us. Or we may have picked a life verse and we can quote it. Maybe we can remember precious Bible promises and calm down while Jesus helps us look at things from His perspective, not ours.

If our brain tends to get foggy in a crisis, why not prepare a 3x5 card that includes the reminders that help us recall our Christian roots? Keep it handy to pull out of our pocket when we see the need to do a drill. Our card might say something like this:

> I became a Christian in 2002 at the Riverdale Community Church and I have followed Jesus ever since then. Jesus said that people like me who build our lives around what He taught are like people who build their house on a Rock. Right now, in my mind's eye, I see myself standing on that Rock. Jesus is here. My Pilot is here. This is solid and steady ground. Thank You, Jesus, that You will help my Pilot figure out what to do next.

When the wind and the rain beat against our house, and they frighten us into noticing we need to do a drill, be encouraged that Pilot lives up in that solid rock house. And the God of Peace invites us to take refuge in that steady, safe place, while He helps us do our silly little drills that restore peace to Amy and Hippo.

April 26: Pilot…And a Simple, Two-Part Exercise

…whatever is true, whatever is noble, whatever is right, whatever is pure, whatever is lovely, whatever is admirable – if anything is excellent or praiseworthy – think about such things. Phil. 4:8

SITUATION

My conversation with Elaine got me to thinking. I'm delighted that the most recent brain research has debunked the old "truism" that the brain stops developing at some super young age – five or so, as I recall. **The new-found magic of *neuroplasticity* has proven that the brain can continue to regenerate and heal and grow new synapses well into middle age or even old age (if we're blessed with good genes and haven't suffered neurological damage).**

Before moving on, it occurred to me to stop and talk a little bit more about how we can target our Pilot for some remedial neuroplasticity if, like Elaine, our Pilot hasn't quite gotten up to speed yet through no fault of our own.

The brain generally operates on a simple use-it-or-lose-it basis. So if you want to beef up the language centers in your brain, for instance, go learn a foreign language. Your language centers will add tons of great new synapses. Want to shore up your cognitive skills? Learn how to do Sudoku® or origami if you've never tried it before, or go learn new kinds of puzzles. Stand-down and Grounding drills beef up our limbic system. You get the idea.

AN EXERCISE THAT TARGETS OUR PILOT

OK. Now let's apply this to our Pilot. The Pilot center of the brain gets strengthened by doing a simple little exercise that we've been doing all along without me spelling it out specifically. It's super easy if you know what to do.

Let's call this easy two-part exercise **NOTICE & SET**.

1. NOTICE

The Pilot has already activated when we notice something about our frame of mind. So the first step is already half way done. When we notice that our mind has begun to notice something about what our mind is doing or has noticed a body cue related to Survivor Mode, we seize the opportunity and focus on whatever Pilot alerted us to notice. We don't notice and then go back to mindlessly watching TV or whatever we were doing when our Pilot interrupted. **We pause and pay attention.** That reinforces the Pilot's action of noticing the workings on its own mind.

By the way, it's not enough to perk up when our brain notices any old thing like a siren in the distance or a bug on the wall. We watch for when our mind observes its own mind or body instead of mindlessly going with the flow or ignoring the direction of our thoughts.

Got it?

2. SET

As an intentional act – key word **intentional** – we **SET** our mind on something of our choosing. Makes no difference at all for purposes of this Pilot exercise what we set our mind on. We can set our mind to **think** along a new line or we can set our mind to **do** an action of our choice.

Notice that we already do this two-part Pilot exercise whenever we decide to do Stand-Down or Grounding. We notice the need to collect ourselves. Or rather, our Pilot notices the need and we pay attention to what Pilot notices. Pilot assesses the body cues and chooses a drill, then intentionally sets the brain to focus on the steps of that drill. If it's Stand-Down, Pilot sets its focused, absorbed attention to each part of each breath, and so on. If Pilot chooses Grounding, it sets its focused, absorbed attention to connecting with the toes, etc.

For purposes of doing this Pilot-building Notice-and-Set exercise, **it's no biggie to get distracted**. If we notice our mind start to wander off in the middle of doing a drill, it gives us a great opportunity to NOTICE that our mind wandered off. Pilot can gently turn its attention to the wandering mind and choose to SET it back to doing the drill.

We do the NOTICE & SET exercise when we get quiet and our freaked out, clueless, critical and mean voice rushes forward. Our Pilot chooses to find and use the more calm, assessing, curious and kind part of our personality (even if that's an underdeveloped voice in our head). Not to worry. That part tends to develop as we choose that voice time after time.

We do the NOTICE & SET exercise when we find ourselves stewing and take to heart Phil. 4:8, the perfect verse to describe notice-and-set. Paul encourages us to **notice the meditations of our heart** and deliberately choose to think about worthy topics and productive lines of thought.

We do the NOTICE & SET exercise whenever we take to heart Col. 3:1 to "set our mind on things above, where Christ is…."

Any of these NOTICE & SET exercises target the prefrontal cortex (Pilot) region of our brain and put in place robust synapse connections that complete whatever part of the task was left unfinished by our particular childhood situation.

So, be encouraged if it feels wobbly at first to find your Pilot. It helps to know what's going on. The very fact that it feels unfamiliar means that we've found a great spot in which to build some new synapses – much better than tackling a new foreign language or learning to play the accordion!

Let's unleash the God-given magic of neuroplasticity.

April 30: Flight Mode...And the What Ifs?

SITUATION

Something that C.S. Lewis wrote in *The Screwtape Letters* helped me sort out my *What Ifs?* and it happened this way. Since Jim and I are getting closer to retirement, we often brainstorm ideas about what to do with ourselves in our later years. We have three or four main options that we've researched and kicked around from time to time. I wouldn't say that we have much fear about this. We've been trusting God for a long time and God hasn't let us down yet.

So anyway, the other day something really minor happened. A friend of mine made a little comment which gave me a frisson of worry. That worry percolated for a few days. This afternoon it suddenly dawned on me that I had mentally travelled a far piece from her initial comment.

Based on that one comment, I had imagined that I had moved to another state, that we had fully enacted one of the retirement options Jim and I have kicked around, that Jim had died before me and that I was a widow who was getting pushed around. My worry today centered on how I would handle what I envisioned happening after all those other things had transpired. It had spooled out so ridiculously far into the ether of one *What if?* after another *What if?* after another *What if?* after another *What if?* that suddenly I laughed out loud.

I can't believe this! I'm actually worrying about something that's four *What Ifs?* out! Is that stupid or what?

I took this idiotic worry to the Lord and asked what I could do to get a handle on these *What If?* kinds of worry. What will bring me to peace and keep me at peace?

INSIGHTS

Immediately I thought of *The Screwtape Letters*. It's a classic story that gives advice for new Christians from an upside down angle. It imagines a young demon named Wormwood asking advice from a devious older demon named Screwtape on how to mess up a new Christian.

In Letter 15, Wormwood asked Screwtape whether the Evil One preferred him keeping his human subject preoccupied with the past or the future. Screwtape commented that **"humans live in time, but our Enemy destines them to eternity. He therefore, I believe, wants them to attend chiefly to two things, to eternity itself and to that point in time which they call the Present. For the Present is the point at which time touches eternity."**

Distracting believers to dwell on the past or the future each have their advantages but Screwtape concludes that it's probably better for their diabolical purposes to get their thoughts focused on the future because:

> ...thought[s] about the future inflame hope and fear. Also, it is **unknown** to them, so in making them think about it **we make them think of unrealities**. In a word, **the Future is, of all things, the thing <u>least</u> like eternity**. It is the

> most completely temporal part of time – for the Past is frozen and no longer flows, and the Present is all lit up with eternal rays [my emphasis].

OK. Isn't that just fantastic writing?

When I worried about something that stood on the wobbly foundation of four different scenarios all coming true, I got sidetracked into complete unreality, in fact, into *the least real thing* on earth. It was so ridiculous, that its very silliness helped break the hold it had on me.

Later on in the same letter, Lewis adds that planning for tomorrow's predictable trouble is an appropriate part of today's duty.

So here's how I see to handle the *What If's* based on *The Screwtape Letters*. Fig. 19, "Handling the What Ifs?" illustrates what Lewis said regarding how to view time. I love his comment that the past and the present are REAL because they have either already happened or they are unfolding right now. My future here on earth is the LEAST REAL. I have no idea how long I have left, which specific possible events will affect me and which will not.

Our goal is to attend mainly to Now and to Eternity. God is the great I AM. Our peace of mind comes when we stay in the present (as "i am" in little letters). I AM with i am.

In addition, I've added an arrow along the bottom to show my actual life from birth to death, and beyond into eternity. I'm convinced that God has assigned me one particular story because I Corinthians 7:17 says, "Nevertheless, each person should live as a believer in whatever situation God has assigned to them."

I hear the Lord's quiet reassurance that I only have to trust Him for the one actual story He has assigned to me.

Fig. 19: HANDLING THE WHAT IFS?

MY PAST	NOW	MY FUTURE	ETERNITY
REAL: It actually happened FROZEN	REAL: It's happening now Only here am I free to act or to prepare wisely I AM with i am	LEAST REAL: Unknown amt of time Unknown events Full of UNREALITIES and What Ifs? ? ? ? ?/? ? ? ? WHAT IFS?	MOST REAL: Eternal NOW where God lives I am with i am

BIRTH — MY ONE ACTUAL LIFE — DEATH →

In the least real potential future we all get hit every day by dozens of horrible-things-that-might-happen-to-you-or-to-the-ones-you-love. As I pondered this diagram in light of my story, I see how to apply it to my story.

As of now, every W*hat If?* scenario gets officially labeled as being part of my Least Real future. Those scary options cannot possibly all happen to me or people I love. This addresses the element of dread.

If something comes along that strikes fear in my heart, I should ask myself: **Is this a live option that I should prepare for in some way?** If I see a story about getting eaten by a polar bear up at the North Pole, it's doubtful that would ever happen to me. And there is no practical thing to do to prepare for that eventuality.

So I can **throw that particular *What If?* into a huge bag of Unrealities I've called the *What Ifs?*** on my diagram along with all the *What Ifs* about various diseases, tape worms, asteroid disasters, millions of Google® search results and potential things to fear. And I ask God to handle that whole pile. My brain isn't big enough to trust God for each one of those gazillion *What Ifs?*. But I don't have to; I only need to trust God for my one actual story.

Now sometimes I do hear about a *What If?* that could conceivably happen to me and mine. It reminds me of an article I ran across about what to do if your car goes off the road and lands underwater.

OK....unlikely, but possible. We live by water and friends of ours did drown when their car crashed into the Gunnison River. The article suggested that if you have the presence of mind as you're sliding under water and your electrical system still works, roll down your windows. If worse comes to worse, make sure that you've bought one of those little Car Window Hammers with the sharp point that can break your driver's side window if need be.

So I went on Amazon® and bought two car hammers for under $10 each. I keep them handy in the car. That makes one less *What If?* to worry about.

I had never before seen the stark choice we face when a fear about the future rears its fearsome head. We have a choice. We can either get swallowed up by the unrealities of the *What Ifs?,* which will intensify our anxiety. Or we can steadfastly shift our focus to the promises that God has given us for our one actual life.

God is faithful to keep His promises but He only does it along that long arrow of our one actual life.

Standing on that solid ground allows genuine confidence about the future to flourish. When Jim and I were dating, we picked Jeremiah 29:11 as the promise for our relationship. Boy, if Jim and I had a nickel for every time we chose to turn away from obsessing about a dreaded *What If?* and quoted that verse out loud to each other, why, we'd have a huge pile of nickels! Repeat after me, **"'For I know the plans I have for you,' declares the Lord, 'plans to prosper you and not to harm you, plans to give you hope and a future.'"**

Today after I pulled out my beat up copy of *Screwtape Letters* I sensed a click in my spirit about the *What Ifs?* Let's see how this works.

May 22: Grounding…And the Stomach Flu

MY DILEMMA

Why did I resist praying (except with Jim) or doing the Stand-Down or Grounding drill while I was sick with stomach flu for six days? Near the end of my flu cycle, I took my question to Jesus, confessed the sin of not praying consistently this week and asked what to do.

DRILL: Tried to do Grounding

WHAT HAPPENED?

When I activated Pilot and assessed body cues I immediately felt flooded by pain messages from all over my body that I'd been ignoring. *Hmmm.* Then my body actively resisted when I tried to mentally connect my Pilot to my toe. For the first time all year, something within me emphatically did not want to align my body or connect it. (My Pilot assessed that my Smart Brain and my Emotional Brain felt calm and at rest.)

I sat quietly and wondered: *Why that resistance?*

Apparently, my body instinctively knew what to do but my conscious mind hadn't figured it out yet. So I waited with curiosity. It felt like my body was telling me that, just this once, connecting the three brains would hinder my healing, not help it. Yes, Grounding would, reliably, pull me fully present to this place. But was that the wisest idea? High levels of pain reside here today. Body Brain would actually do a better job of helping me recover if I just left it alone.

I asked Jesus to weigh in on this odd situation.

TODAY'S SOLUTION & MY TAKE AWAY

In the stillness, He reminded me of a phrase from "In the Morning," one of the crafted prayers in the Anglican classic, *The Book of Common Prayer*. I thumbed through my copy. Several of those prayers really fit my story this morning so I prayed them instead of doing a drill. Later on, I wrote out three of the prayers on 3x5 cards to keep them handy with my stash of stuff for this year of experiments.

INSIGHT

Painful Illness = Shut down (a kind of Freeze Mode but ≠ limbic Freeze Mode)

This kind of shut down is purely physical, the wounded animal curled up inside its den. The animal isn't in mental distress or Survivor Mode even though it's quite injured. It just instinctively knows it will heal quicker if it's left on its own until Body Brain gives the OK to return to regular activity.

Like that holed up animal, the only distress I felt at the start was a Smart Brain sort of guilt at not praying. Regarding the pain level, actually, the numbness felt peaceful. When I brought Pilot on board to assess the cues, the level of pain took me by surprise because Body Brain had been anesthetizing me from the worst of it.

On sick days, short crafted prayers may fit the need perfectly. I felt sweetly connected to Jesus who knew exactly what I needed without the need of collecting myself in the usual way. And praying those prayers I love didn't unduly disturb the healing process managed by my Body Brain. I came away with a deeper appreciation for the elegance of its hidden wisdom.

THE BOOK OF COMMON PRAYER: PRAYERS FOR USE BY A SICK PERSON, PG. 461

Crafted Prayers that Work Well when the Grounding Drill isn't the Best Tool for Bringing Us to Peace

In the Morning

This is another day, O Lord. I know not what it will bring forth,
but make me ready, Lord, for whatever it may be.
If I am to stand up, help me to stand bravely.
If I am to sit still, help me to sit quietly.
If I am to lie low, help me to do it patiently.
And if I am to do nothing, let me do it gallantly.
Make these words more than words, and give me the Spirit of Jesus. Amen.

For trust in God

O God, the source of all health:
So fill my heart with faith in your love,
that with calm expectancy I may make room for your power to possess me,
and gracefully accept your healing; through Jesus Christ our Lord. Amen.

In Pain

Lord Jesus Christ,
by your patience in suffering you hallowed earthly pain
and gave us an example of obedience to your Father's will:
Be near me in my time of weakness and pain;
sustain me by your grace, that my strength and courage may not fail;
heal me according to your will;
and help me always to believe that what happens to me here is of little account
if you hold me in eternal life,
my Lord and my God. Amen.

May 31: Pilot…And the Utterly Different Worldview

SITUATION

My conversation with Elaine a month ago gave me plenty of food for thought and a new direction to explore. Up until then I saw these experiments on two entirely separate tracks:

- the **"body"** track of studying the brain and doing the two drills to calm the body, and
- the **"spiritual"** track of pursuing the peace of Christ.

I assumed I did the drills to calm my body to make it easier to pray and find the peace of Christ for whatever had upset me. But especially after Elaine and I got the idea of connecting Pilot to the Rock, I began mulling over how to more intentionally start connecting these two tracks in other ways.

> **How do I more intentionally set Pilot to start each day on the Rock? Instead of just letting Pilot sort of hang out observing our mind until we need it to manage the drills, how do we "preach the gospel" to Pilot so it evaluates our upset-of-the-moment from heaven's worldview?**

Up until then I had taken for granted that it was fine to get upset about whatever upset us and we took all of that to Jesus and let Him bring us to peace. After my heart attack, Jesus raised the bar to insist I come to peace about more things with less delay.

That's really hard to pull off if I buy into the world's mindset of valuing what the world values. If I hold only vague, fuzzy thoughts about my position in Christ but take at face value to cling on to tangible possessions and fight to keep my status here on earth, how can I ever find lasting peace of mind?

My January prayer retreat had given strategy: if something puzzles me, start looking for the solution in my theme verse and then in the rest of Colossians 3. As I pondered this question day after day, my attention shifted to the first four verses of Colossians 3.

> Since, then, you have been raised with Christ, set your hearts on things above, where Christ is seated at the right hand of God. Set your minds on things above, not on earthly things. For you died, and your life is now hidden with Christ in God. When Christ, who is your life, appears, then you also will appear with Him in glory.

I noticed this paragraph is absolutely jam-packed with positional truth about who I am in Christ and what is true about me because I've become a believer. Pondering these phrases took me to other verses in Colossians and in the rest of the New Testament that fleshed out a great description of the Rock and the worldview of heaven. **Instead of "loitering about" until Amy and Hippo shove us into Flight, Fight or Freeze, Pilot can and should proactively orient itself each morning to stand on these positional truths.**

7 POSITIONAL TRUTHS PACKED INTO COLOSSIANS 3:1-4

1. "Since, then, you have been raised with Christ..." Right off the bat, this phrase refers back to our assurance that, in a way we can't understand, whatever happened to Jesus at the end of His earthly life also happened to us:

- When He died, we died with Him,
- When He was buried, we were buried with Him and
- When He rose on the third day, we also came alive again with Him (Col. 2:12, 13, 20).
- After 40 days, Jesus went up to heaven, so in this mysterious way, we also went with Him.

Every new morning we wake up to the positional truth that we live life from the position of being raised with Christ. Christ triumphed over death and we join in Christ's victory over death and sin (Col. 2:13-15).

2. "...Set your hearts on things above where Christ is seated at the right hand of God..." This gives us heaven's worldview in at least two ways.

1) It keeps our attention on Christ in His glory and
2) It shifts the things we value most to be those we send on ahead to heaven.

"Do not store up for yourselves treasures on earth, where moth and vermin destroy and where thieves break in and steal. But store up for yourselves treasures in heaven where moth and vermin do not destroy and where thieves do not break in and steal. For where your treasure is there your heart will be also" (Matthew 6:19-21).

"Our Father in heaven, hallowed be Your name, Your kingdom come, Your will be done on earth as it is in heaven..." (Matthew 6:9, 10).

"Command those who are rich in this present world not to be arrogant nor to put their hope in wealth which is so uncertain, but to put their hope in God who richly provides us with everything for our enjoyment" (I Timothy 6:17).

3. "…Set your mind on things above, not on earthly things…" Talk about a perfect illustration of that simple two-part PILOT exercise, Notice-and-Set! This verse says we intentionally take our minds off of all bickering, local drama and nearby in-fighting. "And if someone wants to sue you and take your tunic, let him have your cloak as well. If someone forces you to go one mile, go with him two miles" (Matthew 5:40, 41). We quit setting our hearts on our possessions and earthly status or making sure no one disrespects us.

It reminds me of Martin Luther's old hymn, "Let goods and kindred go; this mortal life also. The body they may kill. God's truth abideth still. His kingdom is forever."

I wonder how much panic and anger and anxiety we would completely avoid if we really embraced this idea and saw earthly things for what they really are – stuff that won't last, stuff we can live without, indignities that don't touch our core value, and brouhahas we can detour around instead of letting them drain us dry.

4. "…for you died…" This speaks to the death of our flesh and our sin nature.

"I have been crucified with Christ and I no longer live but Christ lives in me" (Gal. 2:20a).

"In the same way, count yourselves as dead to sin but alive to God in Christ Jesus. Therefore do not let sin reign in your mortal body so that you obey its evil desires. Do not offer the parts of your body to sin as instruments of wickedness, but rather offer yourselves to God as those who have been brought from death to life; and offer the parts of your body to Him as instruments of righteousness" (Romans 6:11-13).

How often do I get upset at people because they wounded my ego and my pride, or how often have I jumped on the band wagon when others were acting out of their carnality, not their better self? To my chagrin, this phrase especially convicted me and I took it to heart.

5. "…and your life is now hidden with Christ in God…" I recalled the insight from back in January when I wondered about this very phrase. We want so much to have all mysteries revealed now. We chafe at limbo and the unknowns of having to wait around while a situation unfolds. I remember the Spirit saying, **"It is hidden even from you."** Back then I had the thought to peacefully "allow the unknowing to be there. It's outside of time and space, *in the heavenlies* of Ephesians." We set our minds on "things above," which orients us to that spiritual self already hidden with Christ, waiting to be revealed.

This short phrase assures us of our utter safety as believers tucked into God's two-layered protective hand. "My sheep listen to My voice; I know them, and they follow Me. I give them eternal life, and they shall never perish; no one will snatch them out of My hand. My Father, who has given them to Me, is greater than all, and no one can snatch them out of my Father's hand" (John 10:27-29).

6. "...When Christ, who is your life..." This flipped worldview rejects valuing any created thing or any person above the worth of Jesus Christ.

"He is before all things and in Him all things hold together. And He is the head of the body, the church; He is the beginning and the firstborn from among the dead, so that in everything He might have the supremacy" (Col. 1:17, 18).

"Therefore God exalted Him to the highest place and gave Him the name that is above every name, that at the name of Jesus every knee should bow, in heaven and on earth and under the earth, and every tongue confess that Jesus Christ is Lord to the glory of God the Father" (Phil. 2:9-11).

7. "...appears, then you also will appear with Him in glory." This final phrase gives the absolute last word for every single *What If?* It settles any worry that things won't work out well. No matter how often I stumble or what catastrophes I endure, He will get me home safely and all will be well. The Jeremiah 29:11 promise that Jim and I claimed back in college will continue to prove true, one day at a time. He will never stop working all things together for our good (Romans 8:28). He will never give up on us. "He who began a good work in [us] will carry it on to completion until the day of Christ Jesus" (Phil. 1:6).

And we add our glad Amen to Job's final conclusion, "I know that You can do all things; no plan of Yours can be thwarted" (Job 42:1).

❧ ☙

MY APPLICATION

This idea to intentionally orient ourselves to these positional truths gives me such joy. Instead of just assuming our Pilot will somehow magically come up with a calm, assessing, curious and kind persona all on its own when I feel the cues to do Stand-down or Grounding, this idea leads Pilot to take its stand on the Rock each morning. It preaches positional truth to our mind, over and over, so that when a crisis hits, we assess the situation from heaven's point of view instead of our carnal nature.

It took me about two weeks to come up with a morning prayer to orient Pilot and a crisis prayer to help sort out earthly things from heavenly things. I have been using that prayer each morning and it has helped a great deal to shift my worldview. The two prayers that follow also include some refinements as I learned new things later on in this year. I present them without comment and as you read on you'll figure out where I added the tweaks. I hope you find them to be of as much blessing as they have been to my soul this year.

Oh, one more thing, Yeah, I agree these two prayers are pretty long. They're designed to solidify my Pilot's grasp of positional truth. I'm praying these cumbersome prayers over and over again until my Pilot gets it. Pilot needs to learn to view everything from this new perspective and that will take time.

Maybe someday I'll find a shorter way of helping Pilot step up into the Rock house of Matthew 7 to embrace all these truths in one fell swoop. But right now, baby steps…and the long process of memorizing the multiplication tables before I can do math in my head.

May 31: Pilot…And Two Orienting Prayers (AKA Two 'Training Wheel' Prayers)

A MORNING PRAYER TO ORIENT PILOT

Dear Father,

Jesus said: "Whoever wants to be My disciple must deny themselves and take up their cross daily and follow Me" (Luke 9:23). That's the longing of my heart, so today I deny my flesh that craves chaos and angst and sugar and resists Your presence and the peace You bestow. I take up my cross to follow You, recognizing that suffering is part of the deal.

Colossians 3:1-4 says this:

> Since, then, you have been raised with Christ, set your heart on things above, where Christ is seated at the right hand of God. Set your mind on things above, not on earthly things. For you died, and your life is now hidden with Christ in God. When Christ, who is your life, appears, then you also will appear with Him in glory.

I'm so grateful this morning that I've been raised to new life with You. I choose to set my heart on things above, where You are, seated at God's right hand. I worship You as the Lord of all, as supreme over all You survey, as the God of Peace and as my Commander. Please fill me with Your Spirit and rule in my heart today.

I choose to set my mind – especially my Pilot – on things above, not on earthbound things because I've died to things of earth and I've died to my sin nature. Please teach me to value the things You love and to avoid getting entangled by civilian affairs.

Please bring my Pilot to full spiritual maturity. Make me a person of peace who faces life with courage. Teach me how to increase my moment-by-moment awareness of Your Presence. Help me do a good job today of capturing every thought within my triune brain to the obedience of Christ. And speed the day when it's second nature to assess all cues from heaven's perspective.

I reject fear. I choose to be at peace about all the unknowns in my life today. I trust Your good plans for my life. Thank You that I'm completely safe and protected. Jesus and I are hidden from harm and we're both tucked firmly under the shelter of our Father's wing. Thank You that I only have to trust You for my one actual life.

I trust that You will abundantly supply everything I need. Because of You I'll make it all the way home and when You return in glory you'll bring me with You. All will be well.

To God be the glory, in Jesus' name. Amen.

NOTE: The prayer below was a working document for me and I continued to add new items all year. Which is why I left a little space under each header for you to add your own tweaks as the Spirit guides you into a deeper knowing of His perspective about your situation.

A PRAYER TO HELP PILOT ASSESS EARTHLY THINGS vs THINGS ABOVE

Dear Jesus, God of Peace,

I feel distressed and upset. My flesh craves chaos and angst and shies away from peace and Your presence. But I choose to set my mind on things above, not on earthly things.

You value different things than I do and view problems from a totally different point of view. Please teach my Pilot how to assess this dilemma and come to peace quickly. Show me the applicable truth to stand on and what earthly thing to let go.

What will bring my heart to peace right now?

Things, Wants & Needs:

"…your Father knows what you need before you ask Him." (Matthew 6:8)

- It's only **earthly belongings**. I can't take it with me and it'll all burn up when the world ends. It's easy for stuff to get lost or stolen. Sure, steward things well but no stressing.
- It's only a **genuine need**. I know You'll provide PLUS give me baskets full of leftovers.
- It's only **something I long for so much I think I'll die if I don't get it**. I choose to trust You to provide all I truly need. If I don't get it, You'll help me thrive without it.

Relationships with People:
"Love one another." (John 13:34)

- It's **somebody else's squabble or pointless argument**. You've given me a standing order to stay out of it because I've been called to peace.
- It's only **my irritation** and **bad mood**. You cut me no slack on this. So I rid myself of grumpiness because You have called me to peace.
- It's only **my absolute conviction that I'm right**. My intensity, my pride and my sense of superiority do not honor You. I let that go. Show me what to say, if anything, and when to drop it.
- It's only **something I'm free to do** but it would cause someone You love to stumble. I let it go without resentment.
- It's only my **offended heart**. I let it go. I forgive their tiny IOU because You forgave me my vast debt. Should I reconcile? How can I serve, instead of expecting to be served?
- It's only **my heartache about the bad decisions of people I love but can't persuade to do the wise thing**. Show me how to faithfully pray for them. Give me a game plan and what boundaries to set. Help me avoid getting tangled up in their drama. I can't rescue them. I trust You to do what is best for them.

My Soul & Body:
"Search me, O God…" (Psalm139:23)

- It's only a **distraction** but it lures me away from Your Presence. I set my eyes on You.
- It's only **my body feeling bummed or sick**. I can let it be, knowing it's only temporary.
- It's only **my ego** or my desire to be admired. That's not worthy of You. I choose humility.
- It's only **sin**. Sin is poisonous and deceitful. It is dead to me. Jesus and I don't do that.
- It's only **my insecurity**. But You love me dearly. I'm Your treasured little child. I run to You as my Abba, confident You'll help me figure this out in Your safe arms.
- It's only **fear** swamping me. I cry out for help. Please, once more, deliver me from my fear.
- It's only **another stumble.** I feel so defeated but I recall Your faithfulness and that You died to pay the full penalty. So I quickly ask for forgiveness and forget about it.

The Outside World:
"Do not love the world…" (I John 2:15)

- It's only **legalism** or a **politically correct cultural truism**. It feels all-powerful but it's actually only a shadow or earthbound thinking; Jesus **is** The Real: "These are a shadow of the things that were to come; the Reality, however, is found in Christ: (Col. 2:17). Help me discern truth from lies and cling to the true Lord Jesus.
- It's only **persecution or opposition**. I receive Your Beatitude Blessing from Matthew 5:10-12. "Blessed are those who are persecuted because of righteousness, for theirs is the kingdom of heaven. Blessed are you when people insult you, persecute you and falsely say all kinds of evil against you because of Me. Rejoice and be glad, because great is your reward in heaven…." Thank You for counting me worthy to share in Your suffering. I choose to stay faithful unto death.
- It's only a bully's **scary threats or intimidation**. I refuse to get intimidated by their deceptive sham that doesn't tell the whole story. "There is no wisdom, no insight, no plan that can succeed against the Lord" (Prov. 21:30). Please give me the eyes of Elisha, when the enemy army surrounded him, to see the armies of heaven on fiery chariots that surround them all (II Kings 7:15-17).

Hardships:
"Count it all joy…" (James 1:2)

- It's only **trouble and testing**. Thank You for giving me the perfect chance to practice perseverance and trust training. I choose to collect myself and face this with courage.
- It's only **an inconvenience or a setback**. It doesn't disturb Your good plan. I choose to wait on You.
- It's only **a random *What if?*** I can throw it on the pile of *Unrealities* with all the rest. Make it clear if You're prompting me to prepare for this contingency. I trust You for my one actual life.
- It's only my **fear of death** or dread that I won't be kept safe. I yield to You my safety in life and the manner and time of my death. I choose to give You the task of keeping me safe and of holding my hand to help me die a good death. I trust You to give me grace and courage to glorify You whether by my life or by my death.
- It's only **tragedy and catastrophe**. I feel crushed by it. But I receive it from Your good hand. "Though He slay me, yet will I hope in Him" (Job 13:15).

June 3: Stand-Down…And the Calm Day

BODY CUES

My body was totally calm this morning but I sensed to do Stand-Down this morning. So I did.

DRILL: Stand-Down

INSIGHTS

I've found that when I sense no anxiety or body cue, Stand-Down is generally the best drill to do. It reinforces a sense of walking in peace and helps calm my thoughts to better sense the "still, small voice" of Jesus.

It shifts the lack of distress (the reality that's I'm in Normal Mode and my Survivor Mode switch has been turned off) into a posture of quietness and receptivity to listen.

June 7: Flight Mode...And Where Tension Hides

SITUATION

I had been having a pretty successful time orienting my Pilot to the Rock this past month but today several strands of worry swamped me. I stopped to do an extended prayer time to pray over all of those fears and worries. In the process, I used a prayer exercise I call **"The Prayer of Unpacking and Resting."** It's a cool prayer that helps you identify and set aside areas of worry and concern, let Jesus hold them temporarily, and just rest quietly in His presence.

After resting for a while, you check in about each item to see if it's something you can just leave with Him or whether it's a legitimate responsibility to put back on again. For the responsibilities you must shoulder, you ask Jesus for practical advice to lighten the load. What will make this more peaceful? What simple suggestion will untangle the problems or help you stay at peace?

(I love this exercise I put together that flowed out of an amazing healing prayer session with one of my earliest clients. It always brings deep refreshment. You'll find it in the appendix at the end of this book starting on page 261.)

BODY CUES

It surprised me to realize how much anxiety I carried. When I checked my body cues, anxiety welled up and welled up and welled up from my chest area once I allowed it to surface. Obviously it had gotten stuck there in a place I hadn't acknowledged.

DRILL: Did the Prayer of Unpacking and Resting

WHAT HAPPENED

Checking body cues allowed me to notice how discouraged I felt about several of the topics weighing heavily on my heart. When I asked God about it, I saw that if I feel generalized discouragement, it points to unvoiced anxiety stuffed down underneath.

Once I settled to rest, the presence of the Lord felt sweet in the room. I sensed Him encouraging me, giving me new heart for this season and kind of chatting over how things were going. It had been getting me down that after four months of dealing with the aftermath of my heart attack, I really didn't have a clear idea what to do. My normal schedule got all shuffled around. I wasn't doing as much of some things as I liked. But in the middle of down time, Jim and I had gotten the idea to put together a book of his blog posts and we had been so happy to get it published. It had gone live on Amazon® about a week before, around Memorial Day.

I also didn't have a feel for how I was doing on learning how to let the peace of Christ rule. How can I know if I'm making progress? What should I work on next?

The Lord reminded me of promises. Again I got the reassurance that this was a limited season of dicey health and wouldn't last forever. Per Psalm 92:14, I would bear fruit in old age and stay fresh and green. And again I got reassurance that He was using the heart attack issue as a tool to teach deeper lessons of trust. He had everything well in hand.

It clarified my task: fight that free-floating sense of fear, especially fear of the unknowns and fears about a schedule I can't completely control. Search out a deeper experience of the peace of Christ specifically to combat that fear and the anxiety – ever-hovering over people my age – if we don't do proactive things to face them squarely and deal with them.

It hadn't been well done on my part to stuff all that anxiety, especially since He gave me plenty of grace and permission to bring them out into the open. I came away more highly motivated to seek the peace of Christ. Fear and anxiety are incompatible with peace.

It refreshed my soul to rest in Him, to talk things over and let His peace rule once again.

9
Helping Others Collect Themselves

Time out for a short tutorial

June 9: Pilot...And Helping Others Collect Themselves

Fig. 20: PILOT FOR OTHER(S)

This morning, one of my clients began slipping into full-scale Freeze Mode regarding a particularly traumatic memory. I could tell she didn't want to slide down all the way so I asked if she would be open to me helping to ground her. With her permission, I stepped into Pilot Mode and calmly led her through a Grounding drill. She really appreciated my help.

I was so grateful someone had taught me what to do because it can get a little tricky to successfully pull someone out of Survivor Mode. I thought of you, Gentle Reader, and figured you might be ready to kick it up a notch when you notice someone slide into an extreme form of Survivor Mode.

Just in the course of hanging out with people or trying to encourage someone on the phone, we'll run into folks who have completely flipped into Fight, Flight or Freeze Mode. It might be:

- A terrified child waking from a nightmare
- An adult overwhelmed by fear, anger or grief
- A disaster victim immobilized by fear and shock
- A group in crisis at our job, church, neighborhood or in our family
- The crew or company under our command or
- A random bunch of strangers

In those moments we either get completely sucked into their drama and emotional turmoil or we can choose to step back into Pilot Mode on their behalf.

After practicing how to step into Pilot role for ourselves, it comes naturally to step into Pilot Mode when we spot those same cues in another person's body language, or tone of voice or the words that give the game away.

Consider this sort of like CPR Training to add to your emergency tool kit.

Some of what follows I learned from books and formal training about Survivor Mode and some I learned by just doing it out in the real world. I know you'll LOVE knowing this if or when the occasion ever arises.

2. Why Stepping into Pilot Mode Guards our Heart

Our training of stepping back into Pilot Mode comes in handy when someone else totally freaks out. It's unnerving to listen to a person rant or passionately vent their fears or shut down into numbness. Without training, we could easily get sucked into their "Upset Me" mindset. We truly want to help them. Pilot Mode guards against their angst triggering us into the same out-of-control response.

Stepping into Pilot on their behalf will help us tremendously to maintain our own equilibrium. In the first rush of their flood of words we can step back to notice our own cues and calmly set them aside to focus on embracing our role as Pilot.

Temporarily being Pilot to someone else is a defined role.

- Pilot is NOT the one who solves all their problems.
- It's NOT the one who must answer their intense questions.
- And Pilot is NOT the one who magically removes the catastrophe they face.
- Pilot DOES listen and stays calm and focuses on them.

But by stepping into Pilot, we stay in touch with our own emotional responses and remain collected. This makes it easier for us to "hold space" for them to talk it out and for us to help them collect themselves in a healthy way without the focus shifting from their drama onto our messy reaction to their drama.

3. Shifting into the Pilot Mindset for Someone Else

#1 GET CALM

Deliberately shift your own visible body posture. Sit up straight and then lean forward a tiny bit. Uncross your arms and relax your hands and switch to a palms up stance. Shift your face muscles into a calm expression and use a softer tone of voice. Do this even if you're talking to the person by phone.

No matter what, don't react with shock.

Don't overwhelm them with your own reaction, even to overwhelm them with your sympathy. The Bible tells us to "Rejoice with those who rejoice, and weep with those who weep" (Romans 12:15 NASB). So empathize and enter into their pain but don't lose yourself within their turmoil. Stay in Pilot Mode for their sake.

If a group faces a crisis, step quickly into Pilot to master your own fear. Then shift into practical, problem-solving mode. Whether or not we hold an official leadership title, our steadiness to address the *crisis du jour* will help the people around us calm down as well.

#2 ASSESS

If someone starts talking with you about their big crisis, they will likely talk wildly, emotionally or intensely whether or not they flip into Survivor Mode. Cut them some slack but keep your eyes open for cues of Survival Mode. Pay attention to their tone of voice, their intensity or their limpness. Watch or listen for clues about their heart rate and breathing, the tension level in their body, their posture, mood, etc. Here are some assessment questions I find useful to ask myself:

1. Does talking it out appear to be working to help them process their raw reaction?
2. Are they staying connected to the real world or are they working themselves up into "crazy talk" at the extreme ends of Survival Mode (hair-on-fire rage or deepest doom and despair)?
3. Best guess, what are they expecting of me in this conversation?
4. Will they be open to letting me pray with them at some point?

I pray silently and ask God to show me what I need to notice. *Please give me the words to say. What do they need right now? Please show me what to circle back to if they give an opening to respond. Help this person find Your peace.*

If we lead a group that's distressed, we do the same kind of assessment, evaluating who in the group has kept their head and which individuals need help collecting themselves.

#3 BE CURIOUS

Actively **listen** to their story. It will likely come in a rush of words for Flight or Fight or in few words and slumped body posture if they've flipped into Freeze Mode. I tend to ask open-ended questions that encourage the person or the group of people to keep talking.

I've noticed from many times of sitting with someone in deep grief or reeling from outrageous injustice, that if I **let them just talk it out**, even the rawest, wildest gush of words usually circles around to a natural conclusion without me overtly directing them.

If they start to cry, **let them cry**, even to bitterly weep and sob. Don't shut it down by preemptive comfort. Hand them a tissue if need be and calmly 'hold space' for them to cry it out. A solid cathartic weeping jag works wonders for many griefs. Amazingly, after they stop crying, most people start to calm down on their own within a few minutes, and often report feeling much better afterwards.

Our curiosity **keeps the focus squarely on them**. If they haven't experienced much grief or trauma before, their own intense reaction to it will freak them out. I might use generic bits of my own story in that case, but only to identify with them, normalize the depths of their angst and encourage them that we will survive. I save my surgery or trauma stories for another day, if ever.

#4 BE KIND

Embody the power of kindness. **Just be there as their ally**. "The Lord is close to the brokenhearted and saves those who are crushed in spirit" (Psalm 34:18). Be Jesus-with-skin-on during their deep distress. Hold their hand calmly until the ambulance arrives. Offer a bottle of water or a cup of tea. Dig out some blankets. If it's appropriate, give them a hug. Crack a little joke to lighten the mood in the waiting room. Pray with them.

Don't critique their words or try to correct their theology at this time. (Six months from now, if they're still mad at God, you can gently help them address that issue.) We tend to vastly overestimate how splendidly we'll respond in a disaster. But even mature believers may struggle or wobble when they get gob smacked by disaster.

Don't add to someone's suffering by the thoughtless misuse of a Bible verse. In normal times, Romans 8:28, in particular gives us incredible comfort that God will work it all out for good. But it often jars the ear if someone quotes it while the person sits devastated, surrounded by their own rubble. So encourage in general terms, especially using verses they find helpful.

And, lastly, **don't hold any of their wild talk against them afterward**. It reminds me of that quote by George Eliot.

> A friend is one to whom one may pour out the contents of one's heart,
> chaff and grain together, knowing that gentle hands will take and sift it,
> keep what is worth keeping, and with a breath of kindness,
> blow the rest away.

Effective leaders show kindness by rallying their troops, not berating them and by triaging to get help for the injured without shaming the fallen. As soon as possible, they praise the crew as a whole and give shout outs to individuals who showed exceptional grace under fire.

4. When should we Consider Leading People Through a Drill?

Trust me, you will recognize the signs!

GROUNDING

Like the possum on our back fence, most people veering into Freeze Mode will start to show some signs of freezing but they can still function pretty well. We probably don't need to suggest a drill for people like that.

However, a person sliding into full blown Freeze Mode probably needs someone to step in and help them get grounded. In my experience, the shift is obvious and dramatic in five ways. If you spot one, check around to see which others have also shown up.

1. **Vocabulary:** They stop using adult words and switch to baby talk or a child's primitive sentence structure. "I scared," as an example.
2. **Body Language:** They start behaving like a terrified little kid, not their adult self. Look for the full or partial fetal position, limpness, lack of responsiveness and a marked lack of eye contact.
3. **Story:** They shift from telling their story in a productive way and get lost in its terrors.
4. **Body Brain Mindset:** They buy into the mindset of Doom ("I'm gonna die!") and Despair ("There's nothing I can do about it. No one can help me"), which freaks them out even more.
5. **Tethering to Reality:** We can see they're losing touch with this time and this place. I call it "slipping down a rabbit hole" because you can almost watch their mind drifting away into a dark place.

STAND-DOWN

At the other extreme, someone caught up by Flight or Fight who keeps revving up into more extreme fear or panic or rage – who doesn't settle down by just talking it out – needs help to calm down. But since they're so vocal and animated, we must do this tactfully so they don't turn on us.

"Do this drill only if actual danger has past!"

One last caution. Bear in mind that Survivor Mode is God's gift to help people survive the unthinkable. If bullets fly, if the Zombies still prowl through their neighborhood or if devastating tragedy has struck, we must be humble in the face of God's built-in remedy. Do not throw a monkey wrench into their body's capable response if the crisis still warrants it.

This is particularly true for Freeze Mode. Dude, if their fragile mind truly cannot handle this devastating loss, or if their pain level climbs off the charts, for heaven's sake, don't drag them back into the horror they had escaped with Body Brain's help! Instead, make sure they're safe and comfortable while they numb out.

Many people who rush in to help hurting people have not developed enough maturity to stand steady themselves in the face of someone else's anguish. **Be very careful that you don't suggest a drill for someone else just because their out-of-control feelings trigger you or make you uncomfortable.**

Take it very seriously, that if you decide to pull them out of their mindset, you have taken on an adult's responsibility.

So, just do it wisely.

Having said that, if you're reading this book, you are probably an adult, or close to it, and your own Pilot training has hopefully brought you more maturity. Your own Pilot practice has already included an assessment of whether to stay or pull out of Survivor Mode when you get stirred up.

All I'm suggesting is that you use that same calm objectivity when assessing the other person's cues.

5. Do You have Standing?

STANDING: def. Status with respect to credit, rank or reputation.
High reputation, esteem

Anybody who flips into the full grip of Flight, Fight or Freeze Mode feels highly threatened and vulnerable. Their mind has flipped into the highest level of battle readiness, making them hyper-alert for any additional danger, including what they may interpret as an attack by you. And remember, their Pilot and some of their Smart Brain got shut down so they can't think rationally.

Adrenaline pumps through their veins eagerly primed to instantly jump into action. And if they rev up into a stratosphere where we feel like we should step into Pilot role with them, we must do it prudently or they'll turn their guns on us as a handy stand-in for the infuriating outrage or scary bogeyman out there.

So, before you open your mouth to suggest a drill, stop and think.

FOR YOUR OWN SAFETY

Do you have standing in this person's mind to lead them through a drill?

You probably DO if:

- They asked you for guidance
- You're their leader, teacher, parent or designated childcare provider
- You're a recognized "wise person"
- You're a trusted friend
- They consider you older
- You've earned the right by listening well to their story today
- You're a total stranger but their crisis is so extreme they grab any help that's handy

You probably do NOT if:

- It's your boss or a higher ranked co-worker
- It's your hair-on-fire husband, wife, boyfriend or girlfriend
- It's an angry parent at the grocery store who traumatizes their child in your presence, but then lashes out against any offer of help
- It's your freaked out mom or dad but you're just a kid (Sorry!)
- It's your bossy big sister or a family member who doesn't listen to you
- It's a friend who considers you a lowly member of their posse, nothing more

It's actually pretty easy to lead a group through all or part of a drill if the situation warrants it and if the group has granted you standing. (For a good example of this, go back and read the March 16th entry of Sharon acting as Pilot to calm down her second-graders.)

ONLY SUGGEST **STAND-DOWN** TO AN INDIVIDUAL IF YOU HAVE STANDING

If you don't, here's a little trick I discovered. Just break the momentum of their riff by suddenly asking permission to take a bathroom break or asking to call them right back in five minutes. They lose their audience. This tends to force them to take a time out to reflect. They often have pulled themselves together a little by the time I return.

GROUNDING RULE OF THUMB

Ask permission of people in partial Freeze Mode. But anyone in full blown Freeze Mode has temporarily shifted into a child's mindset. We have standing just by staying calm and helpful. That makes us the adult. Consider yourself the 'Mom' and just go for it. Gently. As you will see on the next page, even for extreme Freeze Mode, I will ask permission but it will be in a bigger context in which I have already taken a leader role with them.

6. Leading an Adult through the Grounding Drill

It's much easier to lead this drill face-to-face but you can lead someone through Grounding by phone if necessary. When I sense them start to slide, **I speak their name as if I'm waking them up**. "Mary. Mary. Look at my face." (Or, if I'm on the phone, I'll say, "Mary. Mary. Stop for a minute and focus on my voice.")

If 'Mary' is in the room I will gently touch her in some safe spot, like on her knee or her shoulder. This tends to jolt her mind back into the present because I've invaded her space just a little. Appropriate touch helps by giving nonverbal comfort.

I calmly but firmly say, "Mary, look at me. I'm right here with you." It might take a moment, but 'Mary' will lift her head and look directly at me. I make my face very calm and friendly – reassuring without saying reassuring words. (She would discount those anyway.)

I then say in a calm way, "It looks to me like you're getting really discouraged. Would it be okay if we stop for a minute and just get grounded a bit?"

In my experience of working with people in full-on Freeze Mode, no one has ever said no. It *really* freaks them out to get so low. I come in the role of the kind parent to their scared little kid and they tend to welcome that.

If face to face, I usually reach down and **grab one of my feet and just hold it in both hands**. I invite them to do the same. I cradle it and rub it on all sides, saying words like this: "This is my foot. I can feel my foot. I'm connected to this foot. This foot is in this room." Invite them to say the same words to their own foot. (I talk them through it if I'm on the phone with someone.)

Here's why I start Grounding drill that way.

Our feet hold almost magical power to restore our equilibrium if we fall into Freeze Mode. But our person has shut down Pilot and a lot of their Smart Brain so they can't, in that moment, suddenly learn how to do an unfamiliar thing. Plus, they would consider it trivial in light of their crisis. When we trained to do Grounding on ourselves, we did it in Normal Mode with all three brains helping us learn.

Cradling and talking to our feet makes that crucial mind/body reconnection in a simpler way. Plus, it's goofy, which helps to lighten the mood.

We do this to both feet, then shift to squish our toes into the ground or carpet. I encourage them to repeat after me, one sentence at a time:

- "These are my feet firmly grounded on this floor.
- This floor is strong enough to easily hold me up.
- This floor is here in this room and I'm safe in this room."

Once I can tell that they've connected back with their body and seem calmer, I **lead them through the rest of the drill – from FEET to SEAT, LABELS, and MOVE**. I always end the drill by suggesting they **do a simple task**. Usually I ask them to go get a drink of water and come back and sit down. Or clap three times, or close the door, or whatever. The specific task they do doesn't matter. It gives them an opportunity to do something simple and ordinary by themselves that activates their sense of agency: "I can do this."

By this time the person should be collected and mentally back in this place. But they will feel fragile, shaken and awkward. They won't quite know how to transition back into Normal Mode.

Freeze Mode tried to force their brain into numbness and oblivion as a way of escape. We want to nip that in the bud. But the crisis still scares them. The act of going into Freeze Mode drains their body and mind. **They will need sleep or rest** in whatever form to recover their equilibrium.

That's why I don't encourage them to immediately jump back in to talking about the crisis. They could slip into it again. They need a safe way to end the topic for the moment and go rest and recover. I always say how proud I am that they were able to collect themselves and encourage them that they will be able to handle this crisis with God's help and the help of their friends – like me.

I help them calmly sort out practical matters.

- What single thing might you feel up to doing to start the ball rolling to repair the damage?
- Who in your network might be able to give you additional practical help to solve the problem?
- What would be the best way to get you home or to a safe place?
- Who can help you to cover the bases so you can truly rest?

At the end, I generally ask if it would be okay to pray for them. I don't spell out the crisis again, just pray generally that they'll be able to handle their troubles and that God would get them through it

7. Leading an Adult through the Stand-Down Drill

OK. Now let's shift gears. Someone in full on Fight or Flight Mode has an entirely different mental state and capacity to act. Adrenaline pumps through their veins, on a hair trigger primed for battle.

As we discussed, for your own safety, stop a minute and consider what standing you have in this person's mind to lead them through a drill. That's why I always **ask permission** to lead someone through a Stand-Down drill. And it's why I do it extremely tactfully and respectfully.

I wait for them to take a breath from telling their story and interrupt calmly. I generally **ask them a deliberately complex multiple-choice question** like this one, counting off the options on my fingers to make it obvious I'm expecting them to choose:

"Mary, this is a terrible situation. Could I just ask you a question?
How would you like me to help you?

- I'm happy to keep listening if you would like that?
- I could pray with you, if you'd like.
- I could give you advice.
- But my preference now, after listening for a while, if you'd be ok with it, would be to help you collect yourself a little so you can make the wisest decision about how to deal with this crisis? Which would you prefer?"

My multiple-choice question forces Mary to break her revved-up train of thought and make a choice. The act of choosing activates her Pilot.

In my experience, if Mary stops to consider my question, she will become self-aware and realize she's a little out of control. Usually, she will opt for a drill, or for prayer and then a drill. If there's the least bit of openness, I **jump right into suggesting she take a few long deep breaths** and follow my lead and even my hand gestures of OUT for exhale and IN for inhale.

I don't do any teaching at this point. I **act the part of Pilot, and lead her by my example**. "Focus all your attention on your breath…over-tense your right arm, etc."'

By directing her to do specific actions in specific ways, my instructions force her brain to slow down, shift gears and take a short mental break from the ranting or the fear talk. Plus the methodical, rhythmic actions of Stand-Down do their magic and calm her down.

At the end, I **watch for a tell-tale "Whew!"** Almost every single person I've led through to the end of Stand-Down will spontaneously take a deep breath that includes the shoulders visibly relaxing. That body cue signals to me that the person has returned to Normal Mode or to a calmer mental space. I echo the movement with them and we usually chuckle as a way of normalizing this awkward moment.

I've noticed that it will never feel appropriate to the person to jump right back into the same rant or the same fearful talk. So I generally step into that awkward moment and **ask a question in a matter-of-fact way that activates their Pilot once again**. Such as:

- "Now that we've taken a short break, what do you notice about this crisis or your reaction that you hadn't noticed before?"
- "Now that you've talked out how you feel about this crisis, what might be a wise next step?"
- "I agree that you're facing a difficult crisis. What do you think would be one simple thing that you could do to make the situation better?"
- "Before we go back to talking about this crisis, would you mind if we stop and pray and ask for God to give us wisdom?"

I support whatever option she chooses and encourage her to **do some productive problem-solving**. In my experience, most people appreciate my encouragement to shift into a matter-of-fact discussion about next steps. I'll help her assess who might be able to help her through this crisis. What resources are out there for just such occasions? She will likely be more open to asking God for help after she has collected herself.

∽ ∾

Ok, deep cleansing breath.

Before we wind up this tutorial and get back to the regular log entries from this year of holy experiments, let's touch on two last important topics:

- Two comments about helping a child, and
- Some thoughts on how to restore our own equilibrium afterwards.

8. Helping a Child Collect Themselves

Two great things happen when we help children collect themselves.

#1 WE HELP THEM DEVELOP THEIR OWN PILOT

Remember, we said that a child doesn't develop the Pilot part of their brain until around their teen years. A baby or small child has almost no capacity to self-modulate their reaction. They're completely at the mercy of Body Brain and Emotional Brain when things go wrong in their little world. They desperately need an adult – preferably mom or dad – to provide that missing piece and calmly help them get over their fear, anger or anxiety.

We do children a great service to pull them back into peace of mind when they can't do it themselves. So it's crucial that we help them relax and reconnect to whatever parts of their brain have developed thus far.

If a child often feels unsafe, their little brains can't develop properly. They get stuck in Survivor Mode. Remember how Survivor Mode shuts down Pilot during a crisis? Well, the brains of little kids (like Elaine from the April 26 entry) who grow up in a dysfunctional household get shut down often and don't have much practice calming down. That's why these poor kids grow up into adults who frequently slip into Flight, Fight or Freeze. It's the only strategy they ever practiced for handling emotional crisis.

This drives a whole new urgency for us as adults to cut out our self-indulgence and our immaturity. The little people around us desperately need us to take ownership and command of our own reactions. Hair-on-fire anger, hurtful name-calling, unmastered anxiety and obvious fear sets a terrible example and hinders our precious children from feeling safe and protected by us.

We owe it to the children in our care to do better.

So, while I made a big deal about checking to see if we have standing when we think about helping an adult collect themselves, it's a whole different ball game when it comes to children. If your kids flip out, or if you're caring for children who get upset, it will ALWAYS help them when you quickly step into Pilot Mode first and actively do whatever you deem appropriate to help them calm down.

A well-functioning Pilot is more caught than taught. Children learn by watching you model it. And you enable them to eventually develop their own Pilot by calmly steering them back into peace time after time.

#2 WE STRENGTHEN THEIR HEALTHY ATTACHMENT BOND

Babies come into this world absolutely convinced that the people around them will love them, will meet their needs, and will keep them safe from danger. When mom or dad respond to their cry of alarm and provide these basics, a wonderful and robust Attachment Bond forms: Mama well-bonded to baby, baby well-bonded to Mama, Dad and baby bonded in a healthy way. This crucial bond actually changes their brain, creating lots of new neural wiring that will enable baby to go on and form healthy relationships as a functioning member of society.

J. Bowlby and other scientists identified the specific little interaction that builds one completed unit of this Attachment Bond. This entire exchange may play out in just a few minutes.

- "Mom" = "Secure Base" for her baby
- Baby ventures out and explores or sleeps or plays
- Something frightens Baby
- Baby heads back toward Mom
- Baby signals that distress to Mom
- Moms sees the signal and welcomes baby
- Mom comforts and reassures baby
- Baby calms down, feels safe and then ventures out again

Now think about this. **Attachment bonding decisively pulls a baby out of Flight, Fight or Freeze and back into a deeply satisfying activity of Normal Mode.** Experiencing this precious moment of attachment sends two strong, healthy messages to the child's little mind:

1. People can be trusted and
2. I have power to act in my own behalf

So don't worry about specifics when it comes to helping a child collect themselves. Literally anything you do to notice a child's distress and help them – appropriately – in a calm, kind way will reinforce their healthy mindset.

If you have standing to do so, give hugs and kind words, listen to them tell you about their nightmare, hold them so they hear your steady heartbeat, rub their feet, and kiss their booboo. You'll know what to do.

If they had a nightmare, you'll get extra points if you turn it into play time by helping them figure out how they would have punched the scary monster in the nose or defeated them with their powerful pretend sword. And then have them act out that moment of triumph.

9. Afterward: Regaining Your Own Equilibrium

...you who are spiritual should restore him gently. But watch yourself, or you also may be tempted. Carry each other's burdens, and in this way you will fulfill the law of Christ. Galatians 6:1b, 2

As a veteran trauma counselor, normally I can listen to painful stories and help people without any ill effect to my own emotional stability. Because I got great training and because God healed my trauma, I rarely get triggered by clients anymore.

But I've learned to pay close attention after an especially draining session or after I walk anyone through a drill for real, not just for practice. If we aren't careful, we can get messed up.

So here's what to watch for and how to fix it after we help people to collect themselves.

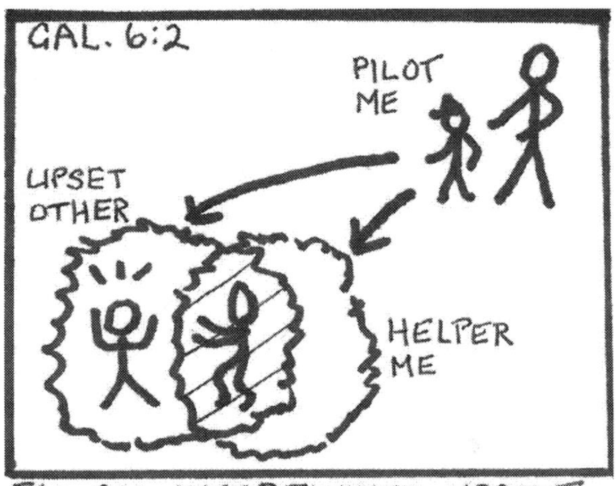

Fig. 21: INTERTWINED UPSET

Since we've been using the mental picture of our little stick figure stepping back from the stirred up self into Pilot, we can adapt that cartoon to visualize our situation afterward in Fig. 21, "Intertwined Upset." Notice that in this cartoon, the Helper Me isn't necessarily stirred up in the normal way. The Helper Me is fulfilling the law of Christ by helping to carry the burden of another. The Helper Me has willingly chosen to enter into the upset of the other person. However, by entering that pain, the Helper Me may get stressed. Perhaps the other person's upset has triggered a reaction by our own Amy and Hippo.

In all four of the actual experiences I'll share in the next few pages, I had gotten too caught up into another person's trauma, as if our circles overlapped. Sometimes the topic of their session triggered me. Sometimes the topic didn't affect me but the intensity of the session drained me or hyped me up. Each story tipped me off that I needed to immediately do proper self-care.

Here's what I've learned to do in each case to disentangle myself from that person's trauma or emotion and to restore peace of mind for myself.

UNUSUAL LEVEL OF FATIGUE

I got off the phone after talking someone down from the ledge, and felt completely wrung out but wired to the max. Even if we like the role of good listener, and even if we normally don't even notice a drain on our energy level, it's unbelievably challenging to help someone in the full grip of Flight, Fight or Freeze.

Do you remember that story in the Gospels when Jesus healed that chronically sick woman who secretly touched the hem of His garment? Mark 5:30 makes this comment, "At once Jesus realized that **power had gone out of Him**." We aren't Jesus, obviously, but in a similar way, power goes out of us when we step into someone else's deep distress and guide them back into safe territory. It takes a huge toll on us.

I can tell when "power goes out of me." I will feel an urgency to go for a brisk walk to drain off the leftover adrenaline pumping through my veins, or rake leaves for all I'm worth or roughhouse with our dog. And often, after the adrenaline drains off I'll go to bed extra early to replenish my energy.

ENTANGLEMENT WITH THEIR TRAUMA

Praise be to the Lord, to God our Savior, who daily bears our burdens.
Psalm 68:19

One time, a few days after an appointment, while driving alone, I suddenly noticed that I had been yelling at the top of my lungs at the abusive husband of one of my clients…for maybe half an hour! Clearly, I had identified much too closely with her trauma and needed to disconnect.

I've learned to use Psalm 68:19 because I love the visual of Jesus daily bearing *my* burden. I value the privilege of helping another person carry their burden for a while. I willingly enter into their pain or grief. But it doesn't help them and it certainly doesn't help me if I continue to carry their burden indefinitely.

In the car, I immediately prayed and asked Jesus to help me disconnect in a healthy way. I did this by stepping into Pilot and firmly assessing the big jumbled and overlapping mess. See Fig. 22, "Disentangled & Sorted."

Fig. 22: DISENTANGLED & SORTED

THEIR DISTRESS

"What part of my distress is actually **my reaction to her trauma** or her emotional messiness, and not mine?" I give that part to Jesus. *Please bear that whole burden for me.*

When I ask Jesus to carry the precious burden of someone's emotional stuff, it lifts their trauma off of me in almost a visceral way. In the long run, it's unwise for me as a counselor – or for you in whatever role you play – to endlessly carry other people's troubles. We demonstrate wisdom when we ask for His help to redistribute the load so we only carry the burden He assigns – a light burden – while He carries the heavier part.

I cannot be Savior to that person but He can.

MY DISTRESS

Whew! Now just by supporting her, what got stirred up within me that wasn't her deal? Why did her particular situation get me so upset? What still triggers me that I need to handle?" I deal with that by asking God to help me process my own insecurity or reaction. If it reminded me of my own trauma, I own up to that and let Jesus comfort me and bring me to peace about my own issues.

BACKLASH FROM THE ENEMY

Brothers, if someone is caught in a sin, you who are spiritual should restore him gently. But watch yourself, or you also may be tempted. Gal. 6:1, 2

One day I got called on to help a woman having a panic attack to collect herself. That very night, I jerked awake in full panic of my own – even though I never get panic attacks.

I thought, *How weird!*

Then I noticed that right after a challenging session of helping a person who struggled with sexual sin I found myself getting tempted by sexual thoughts that normally don't pester me.

After I helped an out-of-control worrier, I got slammed by a worry that normally doesn't trouble me at all. (Not that I don't worry. I just don't normally worry about that particular scenario.) Her consuming sense of dread overtook me.

In my experience as a counselor, I've found that there is no "may" about these verses in Galatians. Watch yourself because you ***will*** get tempted, usually by some variation on the theme of their exact same struggle. Apparently, it's standard operating procedure in the domain of darkness. It catches us right when we unconsciously feel pretty proud of ourselves for helping out our weaker brother. What better strategy to undermine effective Christians?

So heads up.

I've learned to just take authority over the enemy, and run to Jesus for protection. I emphatically reaffirm that I have no reason to boast except in the cross of Christ. That usually does the trick.

COMPASSION OVERLOAD

I know I'm at risk of compassion overload if, when the phone rings or I hear the beep of a text message, my heart sinks because I simply don't want to hear another story. Or if I begin to feel a little cynical or critical about people, instead of compassionate.

These are nothing more than cues that we should do some proper self-care. For instance:

- Take a break, for a weekend if it's normally no big deal or a longer sabbatical if the ministry has seriously drained you dry.
- Gently back away from needy people for a while if you can. Let their call go to voice message until you're ready.
- Clear your head. Get out of Dodge for the weekend and go fishing or hiking.
- Do something fun and creative that absorbs your mind so you lose track of time.
- Go out to lunch with a favorite, non-needy friend and laugh a lot.
- Read one of the *Narnia Chronicles* or *The Secret Garden.*
- If you're seriously running on empty, go to your counselor or pastor to sort out whatever needs sorting.
- Spend unhurried time resting in the Presence of Jesus and worshiping Him. The brokenness of people wears us out. The best remedy comes when we gaze at our true North Star and He refills our emotional and spiritual tank. We regain perspective and reaffirm our priorities. He brings us to peace again and sends us out refreshed and ready to once again be agents of blessing to others.

THE END OF OUR TUTORIAL

Now back to our regularly scheduled program. As you may recall, we had gotten some great insights about Pilot and the value of proactively orienting our Pilot each morning. Pilot has by now morphed into our renewed Christian self, at peace for longer stretches at a time as we adopt a heaven-centered point of view about our troubles.

And then, right after the Fourth of July, I had a thought that sent me off in a productive new direction…

10
The Meaning of "Let"

A random thought one day
opens a crucial door
and leads to fruitful exploration

July 5: The Peace of Christ…And the Meaning of "Let"

SITUATION

I've been pondering my verse this week and a question suddenly occurred to me. It says, "**LET** the peace of Christ rule…" If I am to **let** the peace of Christ rule, what is here, right now with me that I **let** rule me when I'm upset?

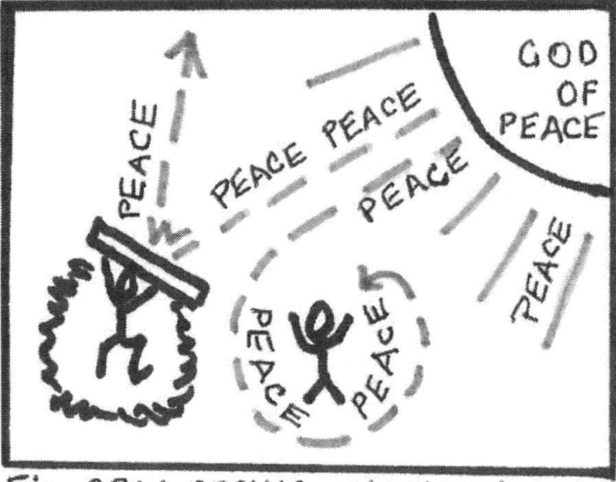

Fig. 23: LETTING OR NOT LETTING

It sounds like, when it comes to the peace of Christ, something is already headed my way…*hmmm*…maybe an energy or this person actively pushing in my direction. I can choose to block that incoming thing or choose to let it flow into my heart unimpeded. It might look something like Fig. 23, "Letting or Not Letting."

I wonder what positions me within the target zone to receive whatever is already out there pressing to be **let** in? I assumed that I somehow needed to drum up peace of mind after I prayed and after I collect myself enough to hang out in Your presence. This phrasing suggests that this peace flows from outside. Duh, of course.

How exactly do I stop resisting it – whatever **it** is – and let it flow down into me? Based on my experiments this year, I definitely block Your peace when I'm angry or when I'm too revved up or too shut down. What more do You want me to see?

INSIGHT

With that question in mind, I checked around in my spirit. The thought immediately came to stop fretting about the problems of a certain client. "Let Me hash it out with her." OK.

And then II Timothy 2:4 came to mind, loud and clear.

> **No one serving as a soldier gets entangled in civilian affairs, but rather tries to please his [or her] commanding officer.**

I recognized the voice of my commander. I just heard it a moment ago when He told me to stop my fretting; no muss, no fuss, not an angry voice but calm and firm. And I let it go.

When I prayed about it, I saw that the God of Peace who comforts so gently when I'm terrified is also this commanding officer giving matter-of-fact, extremely practical orders.

Quiet and attentive, I heard these thoughts. **"I give you enough direction to keep you at peace."** He reminded me of a recent prayer time (one I didn't include in this book) when I fretted about a turn of events I didn't enjoy. "Did you notice how I helped you come to peace? I told you to get back to writing. You struggled briefly, noted how your ego got wounded in that situation, let that go and then found peace in obedience."

Wow! I had not noticed that at all! I've been sitting in this verse for six months focused only on the peace-of-Christ aspect and skating past the rulership of the God of Peace. When you look for it, it's so obvious.

Philippians 4:6-9 also starts out with a firm command to have no anxiety and ends with the peace of Christ guarding – military vocabulary. Verse 8 even gives practical commands about what to focus your thoughts on that will keep your mind at peace. Take a look.

> Do not be anxious about anything, but in every situation, by prayer and petition, with thanksgiving, present your requests to God. And **the peace of Christ**, which transcends all understanding, will **guard your hearts and your minds** in Christ Jesus. Finally, brothers and sisters, whatever is true, whatever is right, whatever is lovely, whatever is admirable – if anything is excellent or praiseworthy – **think about such things**. Whatever you have learned or received or heard from me, or seen in me – **put it into practice**. And the **God of Peace** will be with you. [my emphasis]

I looked at II Timothy 2:4 again and noticed the phrase "civilian affairs."

Civilian Affairs = Earthly stuff

I heard in my spirit, "The great thing that keeps you at peace is the daily practice of doing what I have called you to do, at My pace, in the order I lead. Sometimes I lead you in deeds, in projects. At other times I lead you in seasons of "non-deeds," of life unfolding day by day in hidden ways, the days appointed for you. I keep you on track through the whispers of My Spirit speaking into your spirit."

"You will hear a voice behind you, 'This is the way, walk in it'" (Isaiah 30:21).

> **"The biggest thing that distracts you from the peace of Christ is your own body and fleshly nature distressed by civilian affairs. If something irritates you or gets you upset, that might be a big clue that it's earthly."**

In my mind's eye, I thought of the diagram we've used all year. It was as if He sat beside me looking at that diagram. (I had gotten a glimmer of what the shift should look like back on May 31st and now it fully flowered.) The cartoon shifted a little, into Fig. 24, "Earthbound Upset." I saw a smooth calm circle enfold Pilot and Jesus where we had been hanging in nothingness before.

Fig. 24: EARTHBOUND UPSET

"Do you see it? Your life is hidden with Christ in God. This is not static. There is a life of the Spirit up here in the heavenlies.

"And do you see the turmoil of that upset girl? She's most often distressed by civilian affairs, by "non-peace" and by an earthly mindset. She gets upset if something threatens her possessions or her status here on earth. She's afraid to die and afraid of the future, as if she has no God."

Wow! That's right. Why bother using Pilot to calm down if I keep over-valuing earthbound stuff as if I hadn't ever become a believer? **Maybe it's time to start challenging the premise of the things that distress me.** Is that the distress of an earthbound person striving to protect inherently perishable stuff and her ephemeral status of this world? Or is it the concern of someone whose real life reflects the mindset of my Commander?

Hmmm. Opens a whole new door for experiments.

July 10: Stand-Down...And the Thai Cave Rescue

The whole premise of the *Trust Training* study is that we can take advantage of our normal stressors and life circumstances and use them to learn how to trust God. It has developed a training mindset when it comes to facing life's problems.

I ran across some appropriate words for those of us in active training mode this year so we'll be ready for those crises when our body flips into Survivor Mode – not because of an everyday kind of stressor – but because the danger is actual and real and life-and-death.

It came about recently. A worldwide audience has been following the desperate story of some members of a soccer team on a field trip that accidentally got trapped in deep underwater Thai caves at Tham Luang. It took ages to even come up with a viable plan for how to rescue them. And the solution called for divers at a world class level of training and conditioning. The Thai Seal team divers embraced the challenge and brought all the young men to safety. It was thrilling.

Today they finished the rescue successfully. They saved all the trapped boys and men at the loss of one of their own Thai divers. I was so moved by their story. A member of the Thai Seal team spoke at a news conference. He referred in passing to a quotation I had never heard before. I immediately wrote it on a 3x5 card and have added it to my stash of resources. He paraphrased a quote from Archilochus, an ancient Greek poet (680-645 BC).

In extreme situations
we don't rise to the level of our expectations,
we fall to the level of our training.

July 13: The Peace of Christ...And "Need to Know"

SITUATION

I was walking along, minding my own business, headed around the corner of the church building toward the nursery, when all of a sudden the phrase "Need to Know" popped into my head. I said it out loud a few times and got a flash of insight as follows. That evening, while I journaled about it, more ideas came to mind.

TIME OUT: "THE WORLD ACCORDNG TO DIDI"

When I lead Bible studies, the words of the Bible trump any personal experience. But sometimes when I do an object lesson or teach about a practical matter, I'll say, "This is the World according to Didi," by which I specify that this is just an observation from personal experience. It may not be normative for others; it's just the way things unfold for me. Take it for what it's worth.

You've already read a few examples of this. Tips for doing the drills and my comments on how to help someone else collect themselves drew heavily on "World According to Didi," for instance.

So this is a "World according to Didi" entry based on my own years of practicing listening prayer, especially when dealing with a daunting circumstance or a confusing season of limbo. It may or may not work the same way for you. But, notice that I didn't pick up on how it worked for me until that flash of insight spurred me to go back and reassess what God had done in those old situations.

INSIGHT

During the hard seasons of my life I will lay my concerns, questions and worries before God in prayer. Then I ask, "Is there anything You want me to hear?"

God responds by giving me enough information to get a hint of His unfolding plan or an idea of how to align myself with His purpose for a circumstance. Mind you, it never feels like a ton of info, just a "need to know" cryptic hint.

It helps me relax and gives me enough info to be at peace. I stay at peace when I keep connected to His good plan and obey whatever commands pertain.

In the old days when I wasn't as confident to pray this way, I didn't know I could ask for that bit of a clue. It left me at the mercy of all my fears and worries and *What Ifs?*. But somehow I would feel calmer because He actually had given me that bit of info.

It's like the commander of II Timothy 2:4 giving his soldiers enough "need to know" info to stay on task and not get entangled in civilian affairs.

I thought back to what I have gotten as "need to know" that kept me more at peace.

EXAMPLE #1: Jim and I got a clear confirmation to leave an organization but it was hard to find a new job. We felt unsettled by the long delay until our friend described our situation as a chess game. **Our Need-to-Know hint: God was moving pieces on the board to open a place for us**. That gave us patience to wait another eighteen months. If we got stressed, we would imagine God moving chess pieces beyond our sightline to lead us to a new job. And we would relax.

EXAMPLE #2: I left a ministry I dearly loved and often stressed about what was going on there in my absence. One day I heard in prayer that He had rescued me from a dangerous situation at that organization and placed me in a safe, calm place. But I was bringing all my anxiety and distress into this calm place. **The Need-to-Know assignment: He assigned me the task to learn how to stay at peace here in this sanctuary where He had provided safety.** I shouldn't waste that gift by muddying it all up again with more angst. That gave me tracks to run on. Training my mind to stay at peace during limbo has paid dividends ever since.

EXAMPLE #3: My "Need to Know" hints this year have given me composure and a plan of action during this season of health challenges after my heart attack. Notice, from what you have read thus far, that I've gotten four specific bits of "Need to Know" information:

1. It's a year of health issues related to my heart but I won't die and it will resolve.
2. I should set in place good health practices and sort out some medical issues. Don't blow off the doctors. Instead, handle what they bring up because it will prepare me well for my next season.
3. He's raising the bar to teach me more about letting the peace of Christ rule. I have less wiggle room for entertaining worry, fear, anxiety, anger or discouragement. Learning to maintain the peace of Christ also trains me for my next season.
4. God is shifting around my schedule to free up time to complete this log by December, so focus on writing up my notes. No excuses.

I wonder what you might uncover if you went back and looked for clues in your story. What Need-to-Know hints have helped you manage a crisis?

July 16: Fight Mode…And Visceral Ridding

SITUATION

A friend (whom I'll call Betty) and I had a long talk today about how the two of us could get over our feelings of anger and betrayal after a former friend hurt us deeply a while back. We discussed whether or not to go talk to that person. (Previous attempts to reconcile had all failed).

Later, back home, I went to prayer and laid out our dilemma. *Father, please help us fully rid ourselves of any vestige of anger. Do we turn those periodic surges of anger into clean grief, let that roll over us and dissipate? Do we proactively go to the person even though that hasn't worked before? What word or verse can we stand on?*

March 8 had marked a click in my spirit about anger. I took it seriously to refrain from anger or to rid myself of it quickly when anger surged up within me. By God's grace I have a new KEEP OUT sign that blocks full-throated Fight Mode.

INSIGHT

Several thoughts and ideas came to mind as blocks of insight or recollection.

I recalled one of the wisest things that my mentor, Marriage and Family Therapist Dennis Harris, ever said to me:

At some point we have to say to our own mind,
"You are allowed to process. You are not allowed to wallow."

I took this to mean that, if anger stirred again, God would allow a brief season to turn the anger into a moment of grief but only a brief moment.

I sensed a tender but firm directive: "Dionne, the God of Peace would be very strict to not harbor anger at all. You've already had plenty of time to process your friend's betrayal. As soon as you notice it, go do Stand-Down immediately and renounce anger. I have called you to peace."

So…

DRILL: Stand-Down

WHAT HAPPENED

Right from the start, the BREATH stage quickly morphed into this breath prayer:

"I breathe out any feeling of anger.
I breathe in the peace of Christ."

When I got to the next phase I quickly worked through the major muscles as usual. I checked to see where anger might be localized in my body and found it in my Vagus nerve linked to my heart area. It was weird. I could actually feel anger viscerally although my breath prayer had weakened its hold on me. I repeated the deep breaths, this time focusing full attention on my heart. I would "rid" with an emphatic hand gesture of flinging it away.

"I rid myself of this anger.
I receive the peace of Christ."

At the end I checked around and sensed the absence of anger and the presence of peace.

Afterwards, it was easy to see that my anger had covered up several worries and insecurities I hadn't noticed while anger was the loudest voice in my head. It was simple to pray for these concerns once I had cleared out the anger. That brought further peace. I prayed for the person, asking God to grant them the gift of repentance and to help Betty and me overcome evil with good.

INSIGHT

Colossians 3:8 was the verse that gave me breakthrough: "But now you must **rid yourselves**…of anger.…" I found it much easier to actually "rid myself" of the anger when I did it viscerally through the drill. It helped me to locate hots spots and replace anger with peace. I can be so pie-in-the-sky on the good intention to let anger go. But anger in particular isn't a cute little thought bubble floating benignly above our head somewhere. It's a nasty little infected tick that burrows deep into our muscles spreading its toxic poison. It'll kill you. Dig it out as fast as you can! And squish it like a bug.

July 23: The Peace of Christ...And the Pace of God

But the fruit of the Spirit is love, joy, **peace, patience,** *kindness, goodness, faithfulness, gentleness and* **self-control.** *Against such things there is no law. Those who belong to Christ Jesus have crucified the sinful nature with its passions and desires. Since we live by the Spirit, let us* **keep in step with** *the Spirit. Galatians 5:22-25* [my emphasis]

"Keep in Step With" Anglicized Greek word is *stoicheo*: to range in regular line; to march in military step

SITUATION

In a recent healing prayer appointment, I mentioned a thought that has been quite helpful for me when God doesn't answer my prayers as quickly as I like. I said that I used to get really impatient when I had to wait a while for an answer. Lots of grumpy days. Lots of situations when I stayed revved up and worried and only saw the goodness of God in hindsight when I looked back and saw, "Oh my gosh! He worked it out just fine even though He didn't do it on my timetable. Oops. Sorry, God!"

After way more of those failure cycles than I care to admit, it finally dawned on me that it might be a good idea to learn how to wait on the Lord because, apparently, He tends to do things slower. I could either keep banging my head against a wall and stay constantly revved up by worry, anxiety and complaint. Or I could learn how to sense when His timetable was slower than mine and just adjust my pace to His.

I searched for and studied the many promises that apply to waiting on God. (Some favorite "waiting on God" promises to kick start your own study: Psalm 37:7-9, 34; Prov. 20:22; Isaiah 30:18; 40:31; 64:4, 5; Lamentations 3:19-25; Micah 7:7.)

Holding on to these wonderful promises helped enormously to keep my heart at peace while I waited on God to work things out. I became much happier and more peaceful during the long waiting times.

But, I told my client, I notice that in the past few years my mindset had gradually morphed into a broader understanding. I think of it as "walking at the pace of God." Usually His pace is slower than mine (where the "waiting on God" verses kick in to overcome my impatience). But often, His pace is quicker than mine, or in a different direction than I would naturally go, or more urgent than my level of urgency to do something NOW. Not later, NOW.

I told my client, **"Peace of mind comes when we learn to sense and then walk at God's pace whether that pace is slow or fast."**

A few days later, Pastor Brent preached on these verses in Galatians 5 and a big light bulb went off in my head. Here's a passage that talks about the pace of God that I have intuitively been learning to sense and align to without having a specific Bible verse to ground it.

INSIGHT & TAKE-AWAY

The phrase "walk in step with" jumped out at me when Pastor Brent said that the Greek used a military word for this phrase. That adds to these recent insights about how much the "rule" of the Peace of Christ uses the soldier-with-the-commander analogy.

So "let the peace of Christ rule in your heart" = "walk in step with the Spirit."

Thinking about just this year, I have experienced a mix of fast and slow pace and coming to peace has meant walking at that appropriate pace for each.

Examples of Slow Pace

The Lord has given me the sense that my ***heart issue wouldn't get resolved for a while*** but just to walk through it calmly this year. The "waiting on God" promises comfort me and I'm at peace. My heart event also opened a can of worms of other odds and ends, health-wise, that I hadn't handled yet. I sensed to not worry but just work through each issue conscientiously for the next little while.

I notice that God tends to favor a slow pace when it comes to ***life circumstances*** and our ***unfolding story***. Stop and think: We ALWAYS have something looming just at our horizon that we could either worry about – or that we could stay at peace about if we let the peace of Christ rule.

Examples of Fast Pace

But for most of the things I'm juggling this year, His pace has actually been much faster than mine on a number of things. I had to break into a trot to march in step about these topics:

- **Practice the drills. Practice! Practice! Practice!** He knew I had only two months to get up to speed before my heart attack.
- **Rid myself of Anger NOW**. Nip anger in the bud quickly because I've been called to peace.
- **Beware of the Leaven of the Pharisees NOW** – so no more excuses to worry about money.
- **Stop worrying about the *What-Ifs?* NOW**. God totally controls my one unique story including how and when I die, or Jim, or the others I love. Practice, practice, practice NOW until I master it to quickly cast those *what-ifs?* on Him and get back to trusting Him fully for my one actual story.
- The biggest fast-paced item has been this whole project of learning how to **let the peace of Christ rule in my heart NOW**. I have this sense that, Lord willing, this year provides a tune-up of my body and my attitude so I'll face this next season calmly, wisely and courageously. I have felt such a sense of urgency about this year of holy experiments.

Notice that most of these ***fast-paced items refer to the sanctifying work of the Spirit*** to make us like Christ. They are mostly instructions or steps of obedience or teaching a different mindset and a different world view. From my experience doing yearlong projects for these many years, I've learned that God "doesn't dump the truck" on us. But, if we listen, He'll point out our next project, and all season long He'll give us plenty of grace to learn that one thing if we will let Him rule.

It's much easier to maintain the day-in-day-out peace of Christ when we learn to walk in step with Him – walking at His pace.

July 24: The Peace of Christ…And the Elasticity of Time

As I continued to ponder the pace of God, it reminded me of an especially comforting time with the Lord last December. I felt panicked by the looming deadline of doing the many December holiday tasks while finalizing plans for the *Collecting Ourselves* workshop in early January.

I was afraid I wouldn't have time to finish everything. Doing the Stand-Down Drill made me aware of my wildly beating heart. I sensed Him with me, encouraging me to listen to the sound of His steady heartbeat with the ears of my spirit and to slow down my heart rate to match His.

Today He brought to mind what I learned about **elasticity of time** from the story of Joshua (Joshua 10) when God gave the Israelites an entire extra day without the sun going down and from the story in Isaiah when God did a miracle of time to make the shadow go backwards up the stairs (Isaiah 38:7, 8). God has power over time to make it shorter if need be. Or He can supernaturally extend it to give His children enough time to win the battle or just bless them with a cool miracle.

- "A thousand years in Your sight are like a day that has just gone by, or like a watch in the night." Psalm 90:4
- "My times are in Your hands" Psalm 31:15
- "He shall be the stability of your times" from Isaiah 33:6 NASB

It gave me assurance that I would have enough time to do what He called me to do.

No matter how loud the clock in the room,
underneath I hear the steady heartbeat of His pace
that gives me all the time in the world.

July 30: Freeze Mode…And Dancing Before the Lord

Let Israel rejoice in their Maker; let the people of Zion be glad in their King. Let them praise His name with dancing and make music to Him with tambourine and harp. For the Lord takes delight in His people; He crowns the humble with salvation. Psalm 149:2-4

Let the word of Christ dwell in you richly as you teach and admonish one another with all wisdom, and as you sing psalms, hymns and spiritual songs with gratitude in your hearts to God. Col. 3:16

SITUATION

It was hard to get rolling this morning and my whole body felt listless and apathetic. Grounding got my eyes open but this morning I needed another push. There was nobody at home but the dog so on a whim I fired up one of my favorite Paul Wilbur CDs. I started from a centered stance with arms loosely open and responded to the rhythm and the words.

I love Messianic worship music that blends the Hebrew words with English ones and keeps the Jewish flavor of David dancing before the Lord. I never dance outside those private times, and a dozen years ago when I took my first awkward steps in my bedroom with the door shut to rejoice before the Lord with dance I had no idea how to go about it. I start with the words, so often taken straight from the Psalms or Prophets and sing them to Jesus.

Love songs to Jesus.

And then my feet begin to move this way and that, and my arms catch the loveliness of violin and zither and flute. Oftentimes, without knowing why, I would focus on one hand, loosening it up and saying to Jesus, "My hand delights in You. My arm delights to praise Your name. My other hand…my shoulder…my toes."

The first song this morning traced Ezekiel's vision of the dry bones and the chorus rejoiced to let the four winds blow. It made sense to my feet to face north, then east, then south and west and call the wind forth in miracle power to make my dry bones live again.

INSIGHTS

Doing the drills this year has given me a new level of understanding about several things I've felt led to do over the years – that made no sense at the time -- but truly helped me worship God and find more freedom to trust God and rejoice in Him.

I hadn't danced like that in a long time, and not at all this year. But as soon as the song ended, I laughed out loud when it dawned on me the brain science behind why my dancing had helped so enormously.

Back when I took my first awkward dance steps, I was still very wobbly about trusting God. I had just turned a corner to begin closing the gap between head knowledge and heart assurance. Looking back on it, I'm positive that my Body Brain was still an orphan and I lived almost exclusively in the cerebral world of ideas. My Pilot was utterly disconnected from my hands or toes. It's not that I ignored my body. I forgot it existed.

But when that Messianic music encouraged godly dance, it loosened my stiffness of body and spirit. In an attitude of praising God, it made sense to look at my hand – and really see it – and feel it swaying and following the violin. Chances are, that might have been the first time in ages I connected my Smart Brain to my Body Brain.

The Body Brain expresses itself through body poses and postures, so the invitation to allow the music to shift those grumpy poses into happier ones does the whole body good as it breaks the grip of Body Brain's mood.

I love the way the NASB translates the prayer in Psalm 86:11b-13.

> Unite my heart to fear Thy name. I will give thanks to Thee, O Lord my God, with all my heart, and will glorify Thy name forever. For Thy lovingkindness toward me is great, and Thou hast delivered me from Sheol.

Who would have thought that doing the goofy little Grounding drill would contribute so much toward helping me to unite my heart to worship the God I love?

11
Wilderness and Repentance

I'm ashamed to admit it but
I lose the thread for two months
and then find my way back

Oct 5: The Peace of Christ...And Repentance

During August and September I was hit or miss – mostly miss – about morning quiet times with God. It became very hard to stay tethered to the peace of Christ. I stopped doing drills altogether. Today I hashed it out with the Lord and repented of my faithlessness.

I asked Him if there was anything He wanted me to hear or to bring to mind. Immediately I felt comforted by the closing words of that little hymn in II Timothy 2:13, "...if we are faithless, He will remain faithful, for He cannot disown Himself."

Yes, I admit it. You're right. I was faithless. I'm so sorry. Thank You for forgiving me.

As I continued to wait in grateful but chagrined silence, the Holy Spirit spoke this idea to my heart.

> **"The peace of Christ flows through steady, daily quiet times with Me and, when that falters, by heartfelt repentance and restoration as soon as possible."**

Then He brought to mind several verses that Jim and I read just the other day in our morning reading.

> "...though a righteous man falls seven times, he rises again, but the wicked are brought down by calamity." Proverbs 24:16

> "'Return, faithless people; I will cure you of backsliding.'
> Yes, we will come to You for You are the Lord our God." Jeremiah 3:22

So I ask You, God of Peace, my Commander, please cure me of backsliding as I come to You each morning.

Oct. 7: Pilot...And My Sin Nature

This log entry continues my meditations in these days of personal repentance. Why did I get off track? I don't want to just drift along without understanding. I don't want to let the peace of Christ rule for a few days and then stumble around until I repent again. Lather. Rinse. Repeat. *Please God, teach my Pilot how to assess correctly. What lesson is here for me to learn in this failed experiment?*

Then I had an Aha! Moment:

> **I encountered resistance – not because it was <u>hard</u> to connect with the presence of Christ by doing the drills – but precisely because it became so <u>easy</u>.**

Doing the drills this year knocked down a major life-long hindrance that kept me from smoothly following Jesus day to day. Periodic hormonal or adrenaline surges would hijack my body and flip me into high stress, anxiety, angst or discouragement. I would get swept up into the drama of my body's chemical reactions. It would dull my senses and make it harder for me to hear the Lord or sense His presence in a calm way.

Then I learned the drills and took it seriously to practice this year. **Looking back over the last nine months, I can't recall a single time I didn't sense the presence of the God of Peace, right here and right now, by the time I finished a drill.**

Hmmm. Now isn't that interesting?

I hadn't noticed before, but this year of experiments has helped fine-tune my understanding about the difference between limbic mode and my sin nature. Christians don't tend to differentiate the two and seem to blame everything on "the flesh" or the Devil. On the other hand, in studying the neurology of trauma, the non-Christian researchers and writers seem to assume that inner turmoil can be totally accounted for by the chemical reactions Amy and Hippo produce when they get triggered.

I now see that if resistance to the peace of Christ rises up in my body it can come from either my Survivor Mode or my sin nature.

My **flesh-and-bone body** flips into Survivor Mode mainly because of a perceived threat, usually an external threat. I experience it mostly as **fear** or as a triggered reminder of old trauma.

- "I'm afraid because…"
- "I'm upset because…"
- "What she said kinda sorta reminded me of mom which freaked out Amy and Hippo…"
- "My body hijacked me and I'm caught up in a wave of adrenaline…"

I thought of Jeremiah 2:13 by contrast. "My people have committed two sins: They have forsaken Me, the spring of living water, and have dug their own cisterns, broken cisterns that cannot hold water." Although **my sin nature** can also resist out of fear, it mainly resists, down deep, because of flat-out rebellion:

- "I just don't wanna…"
- "I know perfectly well that God gives truer comfort and help but I prefer my broken, leaky cistern in the form of the candy bar or the social media time-wasters.
- "Even though it never worked before, I'd rather pursue 'peace' by winning this argument and forcing people to see things my way."
- "I'd rather keep control in my hands than yield to Your control and Your plans."

That reminded me of *The War of Art*, one of my all-time favorite books. Even though Steven Pressfield wrote this book to encourage writers, his discussion of "resistance" – a challenge every writer faces – is the best description of our sin nature I've ever read.

It's a cop-out to blame Amy or Hippo when, actually, I didn't let the Peace of Christ rule in my heart for two months because, basically, I just didn't wanna.

WHAT IS RESISTANCE?

A Few definitions from *The War of Art* by Steven Pressfield

(From a list of eleven items I pulled four that most pertain to our situation.)

"The following is a list, in no particular order, of those activities that most commonly elicit Resistance:

- The pursuit of any calling in writing, painting, music, film, dance, or any creative art, however marginal or unconventional
- Any program of spiritual advancement
- Any activity whose aim is tighter abdominals
- Any act of political, moral or ethical courage, including the decision to change for the better some unworthy pattern of thought or conduct in ourselves…."

"Resistance cannot be seen, touched, heard, or smelled. But it can be felt. We experience it as an energy field radiating from a work-in-potential. It's a repelling force. It's negative. Its aim is to shove us away, distract us, prevent us from doing our work…."

"Resistance is always lying…"

The Apostle Paul also knew all about resistance.

I do not understand what I do. For what I want to do I do not do, but
what I hate I do. …For I have the desire to do what is good, but
cannot carry it out…What a wretched man I am! Who will rescue
me from this body that is subject to death? Thanks be to God
who delivers me through Jesus Christ our Lord!
Romans 7:15, 18b, 24, 25

Oct 16 The Peace of Christ...And Going Pro

It is one thing to study war and another to live the warrior's life.
Telamon of Arcadia, mercenary of fifth century BC

In *The War of Art*, Pressfield contrasts "amateur" writers and those who "go pro." Amateurs love to write but they view it as a hobby. They let ego get involved. They talk, talk, talk about their magnum opus but don't regularly sit at their desk putting words on paper. They write when the spirit moves them but don't finish projects. They read books on writing and go to conferences and get caught up in every passing *crisis du jour.* They get crushed by rejection letters. They finish but let their manuscript gather dust in a drawer out of fear. Mostly, they let Resistance block their progress or sabotage their success. Amateurs make New Year resolutions that peter out long before Groundhog Day. They don't do the work. They don't consider writing their vocation, their job, their calling.

Writers "go pro" when they cut out the excuses and just write. Pro writers refuse to allow distractions to get them off their rhythm. They fight and win the daily war against Resistance because they don't put up with BS. They toughen up, buttercup. They serve the "muse," not their own ego. It has nothing to do with finished product although writers who go pro tend to rack up more product. It has to do with a steely-eyed determination to write or die trying.

It occurs to me that when it comes to doggedly letting the peace of Christ rule in my heart I've been thinking like an amateur, not a pro. But Jesus calls us to cut the baloney and go pro. His words from Luke 9:23 ring in my ear:

> **Whoever wants to be My disciple must deny themselves and take up their cross daily and follow Me.**

HOW DO I GO PRO WHEN IT COMES TO LETTING THE PEACE OF CHRIST RULE IN MY HEART?

I can't prevent Amy and Hippo from hijacking my body into Flight, Fight or Freeze from time to time. But I go pro by recognizing that if I'm a permissive Pilot they will run wild. If I don't learn to manage Amy and Hippo, that morally neutral adrenaline will inevitably lead to the *sin* of worry or bickering or anger or discouragement. So I do the drills. No excuses. I pray at the first sign of anxiety and I do not let the *What Ifs* captivate my imagination.

I cannot stop the enemy from tempting me to sin. But I go pro by dying daily to my sin nature, shouldering my cross, and following the God of Peace. I take it dead serious that God has called us to peace. He has called **me** to peace.

I see it clearly in Colossians 3: the no-bull, no-excuses-allowed command to "rid yourself…" and the matter-of-fact expectation that we will put off anger, etc., like a raggedy old suit and put on the mindset of Jesus.

> This is what the Lord says to me with His strong hand upon me, warning me not to follow the way of this people: "Do not call conspiracy everything this people calls a conspiracy; do not fear what they fear and do not dread it. The Lord Almighty is the One you are to regard as holy, He is the One you are to fear…" Isaiah 8:11-13

As an amateur Christian, I let the peace of Christ slip away when I fear what the world fears: financial worries or upsetting situations or political upheaval or threats to my ego or my pride.

The God of peace says to me, and to us, "No more excuses. You're dead to sin. Go pro and follow Me!"

12
A Flood of Helpful Scriptures

*Suddenly, everywhere I turn I find new verses
that illuminate what the God of Peace
has been teaching me this year*

Oct 17: Pilot…And the Knowing of His Will

For this reason, since the day we heard about you, we have not stopped praying for you and asking God to fill you with the knowledge of His will through all spiritual wisdom and understanding…. Colossians 1:9

SITUATION

A few years ago, the *Trust Training* women's Bible study group I lead had done an inductive study through the book of Colossians. Then this year, in my personal experiments I had been gradually expanding out from the epicenter of my theme verse in 3:15 to study how the rest of Colossians built a framework within which to understand that verse.

So when I asked the ladies if they'd be willing to study it again, mainly to pursue the thread of how the rest of the book shaped Col. 3:15, they were gracious enough to play along. Even though my theme verse is not the traditional key verse of the book (three years ago we decided the true key verse was probably Col. 1:18), it has been fascinating to study it once again, looking at it in light of allowing the peace of Christ to rule.

Our study paid off right from the start. Paul's famous prayer for the believers at Colossae, found in Col. 1:9-12, has given us a whole new level of meaning when we see it through the lens of the peace of Christ. I'm excited to pass along insights that have shaped my understanding of what Pilot does and have seen applications for several areas of experiments.

For a few minutes, let me share how the first thought in Paul's prayer fine-tunes the role of Pilot in finding God's will and helping our bodies come to peace.

BACKGROUND

First off, let's check out some of the Greek words that make this verse so rich.

- "Fill" means to make replete, to level up a hollow place
- "Knowledge" refers to an experiential knowing, a recognition, a full discernment
- "Will" refers to choice, purpose, decree (this is a broad word that covers the full scope of God's plan of salvation as well as His plans for certain people or nations in history)
- "Spiritual wisdom" uses the Greek word *sophia,* which refers to the wisdom to make practical decisions. Paul adds the word "spiritual" to differentiate spiritual from carnal or earthly wisdom
- "Understanding" is a lovely word that means a mental putting together, intelligent understanding

INSIGHTS

This clearly applied to Pilot. When we step back and collect ourselves by doing a drill or whatever, and we look around to see how to view our circumstances, Paul asks the Father to fill us with a knowing of God's big picture plans – His plans globally and His plans for our situation.

Fig. 25: PILOT & GOD'S WILL

In Fig. 25, "Pilot & God's Will," notice that, in this situation, our Pilot pulled into Pilot Mode because of the upset, but then shifts focus to pay attention to Jesus giving it instructions. God wants us fully informed of His agenda and His priorities.

For instance, before we decide how to handle this particular upset, we need to remind ourselves that He values:

- People over things
- Eternal souls over our rights as believers
- Witnessing for Him over spending our time on frivolous pursuits
- The development of an unshakable faith over protecting our comfort zone
- Pursuing holiness over pursuing wealth
- Our obedience over our acts of worship
- Pursuing peaceful and friendly relationships over winning a stupid argument
- Bringing glory to the name of Jesus over anything else

When we know His will, we can knowledgably walk worthy and truly please Him in every way. The robustness of our experienced peace of Christ directly depends on our adopting His perspective. Once again, this prayer makes it possible for the good soldier to grasp the clear instructions from the Commander. We not only get marching orders for the day but also a broader understanding of what our Commander values and considers most important.

October 19: Stand-Down…And Why it Quiets our Mind

But I have calmed and quieted myself,
I am like a weaned child with its mother;
like a weaned child I am content.
Psalm 131:2

SITUATION

Yesterday I was helping a new client get the hang of Stand-Down drill. As we practiced the breathing step, I showed her how to move her hands in synch with the breathing. It occurred to me that our hand motion resembles what a good mom does to calm her fussy toddler. The gentle rhythm of slow breath out…hang there a moment…and slow breath in mimics the motion of the cradle, the rocker or the calm shoulder rocking the fussy baby.

As usual, I had already told this lady that we do the drill, not mainly to calm down our speaking mind, but rather to communicate with Amy and Hippo in "language" their child's mind will understand. Babies can be persuaded to settle by such calm, steady cadences.

Good parents instinctively step into Pilot mode and reassure wordlessly. We don't try to reason with a fussy child; we just rock her until she relaxes and her eyelids droop. The calming reassurance at the end of Stand-Down gives words at last to the wordless comfort we have given already: "It's ok to stand down. All is well." It's like saying to a baby that has finally relaxed in our arms, "Hush now, sweetheart, everything's ok."

INSIGHT

This busy Friday morning, Jim and I had to scramble to get to church before I could finish my quiet time. So, since I had some down time before my first appointment, I grabbed my prayer journal and headed for the prayer garden. I stopped to do Stand-Down drill. When I got to the "Calming Words" part, I found myself very naturally adapting it to think, in the rhythm of the slow breaths: "Be still and know…that I am God. Be still and know…that I am God."

I'm still pondering that surprise a few weeks ago (see Oct 7) when I realized how reliably I could sense the Lord after doing Stand-Down.

Why might that be so?

Most people have a hard time quieting their mind to listen to God. When I introduce people to listening prayer I usually give them a heads up that, yes, you will likely experience a rush of competing thoughts and jumbled up feelings when you first get quiet. We discuss strategies to deal with it. Mainly, just expect it and ride it out until things calm down.

Knowing what we now know about the Triune Brain, let's connect some new dots. I don't know about you, but I most often try to calm my mind down to listen to God precisely at times when my thoughts have raced out of control or I feel scattered or flustered.

Even on good days, it's not a case of a unified, collected me getting quiet before God. My Smart Brain is off thinking its thoughts, Amy and Hippo chug along focused on their feelings and Body Brain isn't connected to either of the other two.

So notice what happens when we do Stand-Down.

We give Smart Brain a new, simple job: "Stop what you're doing and intently focus all your attention on breathing out and breathing in." That collects Smart Brain.

We give Amy and Hippo specific body messages of rhythm and breath and muscles to lull them into relaxing and returning to Normal Mode. We reassure them, like a calm mama would reassure her babies: "It's OK to stand down. All is well." And they quietly unite with Smart Brain.

Body Brain had chosen a pose to match its own mood but we give it the opportunity to move in new ways. We check in with hands and arms, with legs and neck by the calm over-tensing and over-relaxing. It loosens our resistance and reminds us of our ability to move or be still, whatever we choose. That draws Body Brain on board with the other two.

When we finish, look at what we've just done. We have "weaned and quieted ourselves; we are like a weaned child with its mother…" In that frame of mind it's pretty easy to sense the Presence of our loving heavenly Father.

How cool is that?

Oct 22: Pilot…And the Unshakable Kingdom

At that time His voice shook the earth, but now He has promised, "Once more I will shake not only the earth but also the heavens." The words 'once more' indicate the removing of what can be shaken – that is, created things – so that what cannot be shaken may remain. Therefore, since we are receiving a kingdom that cannot be shaken, let us be thankful and so worship God acceptably with reverence and awe…. Hebrews 12:26-28

SITUATION

My husband has been preaching through the book of Hebrews, and yesterday he reached Hebrews 12:25-29. It was a great sermon, as usual. Several of the Greek words in this text hit home to exactly the work God has been doing in my life this year. Jim's sermon spoke to the train of thought as I see Pilot settled on the solid Rock of Christ. And it spoke to learning how to let Christ rule in my heart.

INSIGHTS

For years I have applied these verses to refer not just to the End Times, but also to our individual life stories. Chapter 4 in my *Trust Training* study talks about God using the trials and hardships of our lives to shake loose our grip on lesser refuges to give us an opportunity to transfer our trust to God as our better, unshakable secure base.

Looking back on my own story, I see time after time when He rocked my world and everything shook. A lot shook and broke, but as I would recover, I would find what couldn't be shaken.

The abuse of my childhood rocked my world, and for many years it shook my capacity to trust God. I wandered in the wilderness trying to put the pieces together. That shaking shattered my naïve and shallow understanding that God wouldn't ever allow me to suffer injury as part of His wise plans for my life. It shattered any easy believism in God as a cosmic Santa Claus and eventually left in its place an unshakable conviction that "though He slay me, yet will I hope in Him" (Job 13:15).

When I almost died in 2006, boy, did that ever shake my world! It shook my complacency about my health or that death was far, far off in my future. My critical illness shook the people around me. Could God restore me to life? Would Jim stand strong? Would my friendships stay true? (Most did, but the gravity of my illness and how Jim and I stayed strong for each other actually exposed the fissures in the marriage of one couple we loved, and they turned away from us as their marriage fractured.)

Facing death stripped away my grip on earthly things. When you get wheeled into surgery on a gurney, I couldn't help but notice the gurney doesn't have pockets to hold all your stuff! Only Jim mattered. Only our children mattered, only our friends, most of all, only the Lord. And when everything else had been stripped away and I was left helpless, amid the rubble of all the things that could not help me in that moment, Jesus showed up with such steadiness and walked me through the valley of the shadow of death.

I lost my ability to walk all the way around Rohr Park and it still affects my energy level. But I also lost my fear of death because I know in my bones He will walk me through safely when it's the real time, not just a dress rehearsal.

Jim remained rock steady and our love grew more gentle and sweet. I lost my complacency that I have unlimited time left, but gained a deep gratitude every morning when I wake up and have one more precious day of life with Jim.

I gained the promise of Isaiah 43:1-3 during my recovery.

> But now, this is what the Lord says – He who created you, Jacob, He who formed you, Israel: "Do not fear for I have redeemed you; I have summoned you by name; You are Mine. When you pass through the waters, I will be with you; and when you pass through the rivers, they will not sweep over you. When you walk through the fire, you will not be burned; the flames will not set you ablaze. For I am the Lord your God, the Holy One of Israel, your Savior…."

"It's just a wave!" became our breath prayer to handle extreme pain. When a wave of crushing pain breaks over my head, Jim and I brace ourselves, sense the power when Jesus adds His strong hand to grip ours and we ride it out together – steady and resolved and confident the waves and the flame won't destroy us.

SO BACK TO HEBREWS…

After all these shakings, I am left with what cannot be shaken. Verse 28 uses two Greek words that thrill my heart and speak directly to this year of learning to let the peace of Christ rule.

Look at the first phrase: "…since we are receiving a kingdom that cannot be shaken…" Notice the word *receiving.* The choice of tense indicates an ongoing action that started at the cross and our own conversion and will culminate personally when we go to be with Jesus and globally when Christ comes again in glory. We have been rescued from the kingdom of darkness and more and more we experience viscerally the blessing of receiving and enjoying the kingdom of light ruled by God's beloved Son.

This year, sitting in Col. 3:15, **it occurs to me that I have been receiving the kingdom when I allow the peace of Christ to rule in my heart.** Back on July 5th when I had my big Aha! Moment of realizing that the God of Peace is my Commander who rules, that revelation was part of this ongoing activity of receiving the kingdom. Let the peace of Christ rule! The God of Peace who gives peace to us also expects peace from us.

The King has called us to peace. So that means no stupid squabbles with fellow believers, no drama queens, no stewing and worrying about things we know perfectly well God has promised to provide, no clutching onto or fighting over earthly possessions (so eminently shakable), no random *What If?* fear out in the fuzzy future that is "least real" in Lewis's phrase, and no self-loathing, so at odds with the affectionate, true way God sees us.

The last words of Jim's sermon that so blessed my heart also come out of verse 28: "Since we are receiving a kingdom that cannot be shaken, let us be thankful and so worship God acceptably with reverence and awe…."

We respond in two ways, one obvious in English and one not so obvious. First, we respond with gratitude. A thankful heart is the surest tipoff that we really get it that God's kingdom is unshakable. In Col. 3:15 it seems as if the last phrase just got tacked on at the end: "And be thankful." But it marks the clarity of our understanding that we enjoy His peace because He has all power to do us good. I came through the shaking and that's why I wake each morning with glad thanksgiving for one more day.

The second, less obvious, word to study is translated *worship*, "…and so worship God acceptably…." Jim commented that the writer could have used the typical word of worship (to prostrate yourself) but chose instead a different word that means "to serve."

My jaw dropped! That fits so perfectly with all I'm learning this year about the peace of Christ. And it puts such a lovely twist on our obedience to our commander when we view it as worship. When we get our marching orders, we carry them out gladly as an act of worship, a sacrifice of good works, and as the aroma of a sweet smelling offering to our king. We worship our king by not stirring the pot of family disagreements and instead we live out our calling to peace.

Oh, bless the Lord for His unshakable kingdom that fills us with such peace of heart, no matter what gets shaken around us! "The Lord gave and the Lord has taken away. May the name of the Lord be praised" (Job 1:21).

Oct 30: Pilot…And Eucharisteo

And we pray this in order that you may live a life worthy of the Lord and may please Him in every way…joyfully giving thanks to the Father, who has qualified you to share in the inheritance of the saints in the kingdom of light. Col. 1:10, 12

…And be thankful. Col. 3:15

SITUATION

Allow me to continue the topic of thanksgiving since it's been the focus of my meditations lately. Ann Voscamp's modern classic, *One Thousand Gifts*, changed my life and taught me how to cultivate a grateful heart. She traced this word *eucharisteo* which means "to give thanks," starting her study at the Last Supper where Jesus, knowing He would suffer and die within hours, broke bread and gave thanks for the very symbols of His imminent agony.

Ever since reading her book, I have looked for things to thank God for and found them mainly in the constant stream of daily provision, and my gratitude for the good life He has so graciously given me. "The boundary lines have fallen for me in pleasant places; surely I have a delightful inheritance" (Psalm 16:6).

So when our Bible study group got to this prayer of Paul's, I was already primed for a life of gratitude and already practicing *eucharisteo* on a regular basis.

NEW INSIGHTS

Two main insights from this phrase in Paul's prayer have enriched my ongoing quest to let the peace of Christ rule.

First, it's no accident that this mention of gratitude concludes the command to let the peace of Christ rule. The habit of daily gratitude shapes the way we view life and sets the stage for us to respond well to new twists and turns in our unfolding story.

In fact, we can't really obey the instruction to let the peace of Christ rule if we don't also practice daily gratitude for all God has already done. A thankful heart can remain at peace in the face of new uncertainties because it has watched God turn previous calamities to blessing. *Eucharisteo* gives us equilibrium and calm because we have already decided that God is good, no matter the *crisis du jour.*

An ungrateful or grumbling spirit nitpicks and criticizes what God allows us to encounter. It doesn't let God rule, but fights against God and gets angry at Him. That's why an ungrateful heart finds no peace. Ingratitude prevents it from settling down long enough to allow for peace to rule.

Second, Paul's prayer in Colossians 1 points to a specific topic of daily gratitude. We joyfully give thanks for all God did to win our salvation and we give thanks for all Jesus is. We don't stop thanking God for food and clothing and daily provision. But we also don't stop at only thanking God for those earth-bound things.

In just the few verses that follow Colossians 1:12, Paul thanks God for six specific aspects of our salvation:

- that God qualified us to receive salvation
- that He rescued us from the dominion of darkness
- that He brought us into the kingdom of light
- that He allowed us to share in the inheritance of the saints
- that He redeemed us
- that He has forgiven us

As you study the rest of Colossians 1, you find many more things to thank Jesus for and even more aspects of our salvation in which to rejoice. This is a new thought to me, especially as I fine-tune my orienting prayer for Pilot.

It's good to know good doctrine, especially about our salvation and our new position in Christ because of all that Jesus accomplished for us. But just knowing dry doctrine is not enough. **I see that we stay tethered, in a practical way, to the transforming power of that positional truth mainly by our gratitude.**

A thankful heart cures many fears.
My Aunt Ruthie

13
Writing as Archeology

The delightful task of typing and refining
my log notes connects many dots
in my understanding, and
unifies these two streams of experiments
into one harmonious pursuit
of the peace of Christ

Oct. 31: Pilot...And How Writing Doubles the Insights

SITUATION

All year long I've immersed myself in these experiments and scribbled notes in a log book. The last several months I've been typing up the notes so I'll be able to share the results.

Today I had a wonderful day of writing. For weeks I had struggled to figure out how to organize the log entries. When I finally sorted that out, a bunch of things fell into place that left me free to write and write.

Typing up these notes has shown me trends I didn't notice at the time.

It caused an explosion of new insights.

Repentance held the key. It reshuffled the whole deck of how I was thinking about the peace of Christ and it's like I just walked right into this new understanding of how those little drills fit in and supported the more important learning process of letting the peace of Christ rule.

GRATITUDE

Thank You, God, for doubling my blessings by the simple action of typing up what I've already written. Ideas that have floated around in my head begin to land and coalesce into new understanding.

These past few weeks I've seen how pointedly You helped me build that solid ground for Pilot to stand on. These days when I notice my body cues, the mindset I use to assess my situation has begun to shift into this solid footing of my position in Christ.

It is SO MUCH EASIER to find that calm Pilot self when I'm collecting myself from the point of view of being seated with Christ, deeply loved, cared for in every moment and for every need, hidden in Your protective hands so that worries and *What Ifs?* don't pierce clear down to my core. I love being able to simply sidestep some worries altogether since they're obviously only earthbound concerns.

I love writing. I love sensing Your Spirit hovering over me and pushing me to go deeper than the first draft log entry. It reminds me of an idea I ran across from Kim Edwards who wrote *The Memory Keeper's Daughter*:

> For me, writing is never linear, although I do believe quite ardently in revision. I think of revision as a kind of archeology, a deep exploration of the text to discover what's still hidden and bring it to the surface.

That hits on what I've enjoyed so much – doing the archeology – bringing what's still hidden in the text – hidden from me and from the readers – out into the daylight where it can bless us all.

Nov. 3: Fight Mode...And Fretting as Resistance

SITUATION

What is it about doing the laundry on Saturday that gets me into fretting? I had been so pleased with myself for having more control of those thoughts. I was looking forward to writing between loads but then got sidetracked into fretting about some stupid little irritating situation. Thirty minutes went by as I got myself more and more worked up.

When my Pilot noticed, I stopped and did Stand-Down.

DRILL: Stand-Down

WHAT HAPPENED

Stand-Down worked well to reset my focus. I remembered the commands in Colossians 3 to "Rid yourself…of anger…" and the imagery of *putting off* and *putting on*. Early on in the "Breath" portion of today's drill, I incorporated that idea into my inhales and exhales.

"I breathe in the peace of Christ. I breathe out my anger."
"I breathe in the peace of Christ. I rid myself of anger."

When I turned to muscles, in the cadence of over-tensing I saw it as gathering my ability again and instead of gently over-relaxing, I used a throwing motion as if I was getting rid of something icky.

"I gather my ability to write. I expel any distraction to writing.
I gather my ability to write. I reject this anger."

Afterwards, it was easy to sense the presence of Christ as my commander, pleased with me and on board with my impulse to get back to work; back to the work of writing, and more importantly, back to letting the peace of Christ rule in my heart, even on Saturdays when I do laundry.

It reminded me of Resistance and another Pressfield quote I love from *The War of Art*:

> **The working artist will not tolerate trouble in her life because she knows trouble prevents her from doing her work. The working artist banishes from her world all sources of trouble. She harnesses the urge for trouble and transforms it in her work.**

Nov. 5: Pilot...And the Solidness of Air

SITUATION

It has been a profitable source of new insight to ponder the confluence of my Colossians 1 study, *The War of Art* and my Peace of Christ experiments. I finished re-reading *The War of Art* and saw a new thing.

Having spent most of his book describing resistance and how to conquer it, Pressfield turns his attention to what happens after you go pro. Once you win the battle over resistance and develop the warrior's mindset, a curious thing happens. You sit your butt in the chair to write, no excuses, and then the Muse shows up!

I enjoyed his discussion of the difference between what he calls the ego (that produces resistance) and the deeper, more spiritual self (that creates). He describes the time he had a vision of an eagle – feeling what the eagle feels and seeing what the eagle sees. For the first time, he experienced what flying feels like from the eagle's point of view. He sensed the air beneath the wings as if it was "…as solid as the water feels when you row in it with an oar."

He asked the eagle what it meant and the eagle replied, "You're supposed to learn that things you think are nothing, as weightless as air, are actually powerful substantial forces, as real and as solid as earth."

He concluded, "I believed the eagle. I got the message. How could I not? I had felt the solidness of air."

INSIGHTS

My mentor, Dennis Harris, talks about quantum physics and God's omnipresence. I see the glorious description of Jesus in Col. 1:15-20 and how "…in Him all things hold together."

I pondered those words as I drifted off to sleep. Almost at the last moment I felt jolted awake and sensed Your presence and a block of thoughts.

You have called me to a life lived in Your presence, a lovely and precious call but ephemeral as mist. And, much like Elaine (see April 26), often my Pilot has felt as if it was stepping back up into thin air.

This year has served to solidify the ***groundedness*** of that action. Lately, I step back into Pilot and find:

- The solid Rock of the Sermon on the Mount
- The secure base of my Abba Father's welcoming embrace
- The calm oasis where the God of Peace dwells
- The headquarters of my brilliant Commander
- The wellspring of creativity that pulsates in the presence of Creator God
- The protective Crag that shelters my vulnerable Rock Rabbit (Prov. 30:26)
- The strong Tower to which the righteous run and always find safety (Proverbs 18:10)

I've spent years wondering how to live in Your presence, given that I still sometimes revert to feral cat to my chagrin. I'm still bridging the gap between what I know as head knowledge and what I rest in as heart assurance. In the same way I work hard to preach the gospel known by Pilot to my unruly Amy, Hippo and Body Brain.

Back in January, I called my workshop "Collecting Ourselves." What a good goal to collect the three brains and master fear! What grace I see that You also used this year to teach me deeper lessons on how to live in Your presence.

I collect myself by faith, present my collected being before You, ever invisible and inaudible, and begin to sense the solidness of air.

Nov. 11: Freeze Mode…And Vast Stores of Strength

And we pray this in order that you may live a life worthy of the Lord and may please Him in every way:
1) Bearing fruit in every good work;
2) Growing in the knowledge of God;
3) ***Being strengthened with all power according to His glorious might so that you may have great endurance and patience,*** *and*
4) Joyfully giving thanks to the Father, who has qualified you to share in the inheritance of the saints in the kingdom of light. Col. 1:10, 11 [my emphasis and added numbering]

INSIGHT

Still pondering Paul's prayer in Colossians 1, this past week I've been focusing on item #3 of his prayer list. Three of the things on this list (Item #1, 2 and 4) require overt action on our part. We go out and bear fruit. We pursue intimacy with God – not just learning Bible verses or going to church, but deeper, relational friendship. And we cultivate a thankful heart that enjoys praising God for His mercies and the elements of our salvation.

However, notice that Paul chose passive tense for item #3: "…**being** strengthened…" Basically, the thing that pleases God when we get overwhelmed by troubles focuses NOT on how we gather our own strength and sort it out. No, it pleases God when we cry out in prayer and ask for His strength. We let God pour out of His own mighty strength to help us deal with that trouble.

This lovely receptivity to allow God to empower us also shows up in Col. 3:15 as well: "**Let** the peace of Christ rule in your hearts…." In both passages, we obey by letting go of the steering wheel and allowing God to give us what He would love to give. He would love to share His own power with us and He would love to give us His own peace – if we would just let Him.

Passive tense seems especially appropriate when we fall into Freeze Mode. We're already so passive it's hard to find a pulse! Freeze Mode scares us by its overwhelming sense that we have no strength to deal with whatever has terrified us.

Freeze Mode often accompanies depression or severe discouragement. And that reminds me of Dennis Harris again, who defines depression this way:

> **Depression:**
> The perception that the problems I face
> exceed the resources I have to cope with them…
> so what's the use?

As someone who used to have bouts of depression that lasted months or years, I would never throw any stones. Depression can come for many reasons and some people are especially vulnerable to discouragement. The poor little Body Brain does the only thing it knows to do when it shuts us down. Sometimes the Grounding drill doesn't help much when hormonal or chemical imbalances have caused the depression.

But when it helps, Grounding works its magic. By the time we conclude with gawky bird steps to the cadence of "By my God I can scale a wall," we have reconnected to the very hopeful idea that someone out there CAN help us and would be DELIGHTED to help us. And when we are at our weakest, we can truly please God by allowing Him to fill our frail bodies with fresh strength.

GRATITUDE

Thank You, God, for Your strength and empowerment that always flows toward us. Thank You for knowing our limitations; for remembering that we are but dust. Thank You for realizing that we won't be able to handle graciously all the little irritations or all the overwhelming crush of circumstances or people without the help You offer.

Thank You that it pleases You when we get out of the way and simply let the living water of Your mighty strength flow unimpeded through our days. I can enjoy peace knowing that just beyond my sightline You have stockpiled an unlimited supply of strength (Psalm 31:19). Your mercies are new every morning.

Thank You for the many times I have awakened with no energy and cried out to You, *"O Lord, be my strength when I have no strength."* You always answered that prayer immediately, even on my worst low energy days, and I'm grateful.

Thank You for using Paul's story of the thorn in the flesh to flip my understanding of how this works. Again, more times than I can number I've expressed trust that Your grace would be sufficient and Your power made perfect in my weakness. And it always was.

This morning, Praise God, I woke with good energy. Today I rejoice in the realization that Your lavish strength comes my way every morning. It pleases Your generous heart when I gladly fling wide my heart to receive today's manna.

I love that when we receive Your strength You count our holy passivity as evidence of our living a life worthy of the Lord.

With David I say, "I love You, O Lord, my strength" (Psalm 18:1).

Nov. 13: Grounding…And Connecting the Dots

…being strengthened with all power according to His glorious might… Col. 1:11

SITUATION

I woke to a precious full day to write but struggled to wake up and get going. After Jim left for the office, I pulled out my prayer journal and started my quiet time. By now, I felt more organized and collected, and welcomed an opportunity to do the Grounding drill. This was the first time of doing it after my insights about the availability of God's power and the groundedness of Pilot. It completely shifted the entire drill in a really cool way.

DRILL: Grounding

WHAT HAPPENED

FEET: As I expected, it was easy to connect my Pilot to my toes but, when I squished my toes into the carpet, I felt the visceral connection to Pilot's ground, not just this carpet. I am securely rooted in the love of Christ. Wow! Didn't expect that turn of events.

SEAT: Sat full back into my chair and pulled up my spine with my upraised arms but then stretched out my arms wide and free and full of joy. I stood up and raised my arms upwards again and spoke the words that so often come to mind when I do SEAT: "Thou, O Lord, art a shield about me, my glory and the One who lifts my head" (Psalm 3:3 NASB). I sensed You right here with power and blessing, lifting my head with such tenderness.

LABELS: Still standing and looking around the room, I gave You thanks for all the blessings and delights of this room, the paintings I love, the restful colors, the house plant that thrives in the corner, the gifts and the treasured friends who gave them, and the faith reminder from the year I sat in the story of Mary and Gabriel. I read it out loud and savor the words, "BLESSED is she who has BELIEVED that what the Lord has said to her will be accomplished" (Luke 1:45). I do believe that You will fulfill Your good word to me and I rejoice that You already have.

MOVE: I sat and flexed my feet and calves and sensed Your abundant strength all around this room. *Thank You that I can move.* This time as I flexed one and then the other, I switched to rejoicing that Your strength is here. When I got up to do my flexed steps I received Your strength into my muscles and then shifted with new insight into the words, "By my God I can scale a wall. By my God I can scale a wall." I saw Your strength filling my muscles and I gloried in my ability to scale today's wall. I presented my collected self to You, so present already in Your Col. 1:11 power this morning.

INSIGHTS

Back in January, when these experiments began, I mentally lived in the interior world of ideas and the intangibles of a walk with God that deeply satisfied but tended to ignore my body. So, like an artist who lets her kids run wild while she paints, my own Amy and Hippo and Body Brain often sabotaged my progress. Even though I much preferred the rich interior world of the mind, it remained maddeningly insubstantial. I struggled to make solid progress.

Then I got this assignment to focus on body cues and track the exact spots where my body experienced fear, anger or exhaustion so I can choose which silly little drill to counterbalance.

Instead of an insubstantial free-floating anxiety that eludes the artist's cerebral control, these drills helped me to find the anxiety lodged in my neck or the spot in front of my heart or the anger clenching my left fist. Over and over again this year these drills have helped me to get to know "my kids" and learn how to teach them some manners.

I assumed this would help me sort out the kids so I could get back to the life of the mind where I felt more at home.

And then a funny thing happened.

Stepping up into the empty air of Pilot helped me find solid ground for the life of my mind. The foolishness of the Grounding drill taught my body how to grasp and receive the ethereal promise of abundant strength from the Colossians 1 prayer.

No question about it, my "kids" – Amy and Hippo – needed to learn to behave. But my artist needed to learn that even the interior world of ideas, where creativity happens, needs the nourishment and stability of the collected body.

It reminds me of when I finished up the years of training to become a counselor and had my full tool kit of training and techniques. I felt confident that when I sat with someone I had a map in my head of what needed to happen.

One day I heard an odd question in my mind, "Are you willing to allow Me to work beyond the grid of what you can understand with your rational mind?"

"*Hmmm.* Yes," I replied.

He taught me to rest in the unknowing when I could see something potentially good happening in the client who veered off from the game plan in my textbook as they waited in silence while the Spirit hovered over their story.

This lesson expands on that theme. God fashioned me to feel more at home in that rich interior world of the mind and the spirit. My ears have been opened to the heavenly voice who speaks mainly to the artist in me. And again He speaks to my spirit this morning, this time inviting me to welcome Incarnate, human Jesus who blesses the body cues.

This morning He chose to work beyond the grid of what my rational mind could grasp, and deposited strength for the day in my actively clenched calves. I cannot fully grasp the peace of Christ by mind or spirit alone. Jesus, seated in heaven with His actual, scarred, flesh-and-bone hand, sent peace as His gift for me to locate in my relaxed neck or my heart at peace or my toes squishing the carpet.

Nov. 21: Stand Down…And My 4th MRI

SITUATION

The Radiology Tech had positioned my body on the table, set up the IV connection in prep for the contrast dye, given me the squeeze thingy in case I needed to call for help, positioned the plastic MRI paraphernalia over my torso and strapped it all down snugly. As the table slid me past the mouth of the machine into that tight tube and I lost track of the room behind, I heard in my head, "Hidden with Christ in God," and immediately relaxed.

All I had learned this year came flooding back in a wave of reassurance. I no longer felt the least twinge of claustrophobia from the scratched up tan tube, and suddenly felt cocooned by His protective hands. I have been connecting that phrase to the unknowns of my story. Waiting here in this tube, confronted inescapably with the unknowns of my health issues, I felt completely safe.

I had assumed I would use Grounding mostly because of getting strapped onto the table with no way of escape. I was all set to mainly focus on toes for the next thirty minutes. But assessing my body cues, it quickly became obvious that Stand-Down would help me more this time around.

Oh, this MRI was a follow-up to see if I had any torn arteries around my kidneys. In April and May when I did the other three MRIs on heart, carotid and kidneys, the kidneys were the only questionable spot.

BODY CUES

Mildly nervous, breathing normally but more on the shallow side, back aching from the weird positioning on the table that I noticed throughout the test, mild headache after they hit me with the contrast dye but not too bad.

DRILL: Did mainly Stand-Down

WHAT HAPPENED

Hearing the phrase, "hidden with Christ in God," shifted my mindset into a sense of gratitude for God's protection. That immediately calmed me down. It was easy to entrust the test results to God. I sensed His presence helping me during the whole test.

I wasn't bothered by all the loud banging noises of the machine because I had done it before, but every time I start an MRI test, it takes a few minutes to remember that it needn't bother me.

The hardest part of doing an MRI is holding your breath for a long time. Will I be able to make it last? It always seems like I can't take in a full breath squeezed as I am into the tiny tube.

I saw a huge difference and a measurable improvement in my ability to focus completely on the breaths without getting nervous and in being able to hold deeper breaths for a long time. Practice, practice, practice of longer, focused breathing this year made it simple to control my breath in crunch time.

And I noticed that if I took deeper breaths during the down times between the held breaths, it increased my ability to take deeper breaths that I could hold comfortably.

A well-developed Pilot helped so much. I noticed more body cues and spotted them with serenity, not anxiety. Before this year, I wouldn't have been too clued in to my heart beat. This time around I could feel the heartbeat clear as a bell during the long-held breaths. It pleased me that it remained slow and steady. Periodically I would check toes and neck tension and did minor toe wiggling or deliberate relaxing as needed.

I've always found it helpful to count the seconds or the machine bangs during the time I hold my breath. This time around I felt calmer about counting and felt glad it gave my Pilot a great thing to focus on instead of worrying about whether I'd run out of air.

This MRI turned into a little pop quiz for my experiments this year and it felt so cool to see measurable improvement.

Nov. 26: Stand Down…And Functional Atheism

Peace I leave with you; My peace I give you. I do not give to you as the world gives. Do not let your hearts be troubled and do not be afraid. John 14:27

SITUATION

This morning I woke with this verse ringing in my ear, as if I had been pondering each phrase while I slept and woke from a discussion already well along. A few days ago, I had an interesting conversation with an atheist who was familiar with the drills and found them somewhat helpful. As we talked back and forth it became obvious that she struggled to know what to do after she finished the drills.

NEW INSIGHT

It's all well and good to collect ourselves so we have all our wits about us to make better decisions. And we do make better decisions when our pre-frontal cortex has been activated and we've calmed down a bit. Positive self-talk beats self-loathing and a calm outlook beats panic.

But then what?

An atheist has no answers, but only Hallmark™ platitudes about "the universe" or good luck or "good energy." An atheist concludes the drills by coming – fully collected – back to an empty room and a solitary now.

The drills provide a classic example of peace "the world gives:" somewhat helpful for collecting ourselves, but completely inadequate to settle the *What Ifs*? or the actual hazards ahead in our terrifying tomorrows.

And it struck me how many of us Christians fall so far short when we encounter various fears and worries. Most Christians don't even take advantage of the world's peace, let alone the blessed riches found in knowing Jesus.

I remember years ago, my husband heard an amazing preacher named E.V. Hill. We would seek out radio broadcasts or tapes and listen to his sermons again and again. This morning I thought of a sermon he preached on worry. He set the stage talking about Christians who get all upset and buffeted by fears and who stay agitated and on edge. He asked a great question in his booming, black drawl:

"Don't they have no shepherd?"

Yes. We do. And this year when I'm present and collected at the end of the drills, I've found Jesus here, my good Shepherd who knows me better than I know myself and who personally walks me through each situation, even through the valley of the shadow of death.

Our Jesus is the Alpha and the Omega, the Beginning and the End, the One who holds the future, and the One who delights in caring for His own.

For so long I was a functional atheist who didn't even know how to calm my body. Last week we sat around the Thanksgiving table and remembered God's faithfulness. I was most thankful for this year of experiments that gave me the best the world has to offer but went so far beyond to help me win the full blessing of the peace Christ gives that the world knows nothing about.

All my firm ground – combating the *What Ifs*?, neutralizing fears and learning the soldier mindset, all of it – rests securely on the fundamental goodness of a personal God who rules the future as well as the present. The God of Peace knows my story, knows what lies ahead and how to prepare me for it, and comforts me each step of the way.

When I learned about listening prayer I lost the sensation of ever being alone. How could I ever be alone? Jesus is always here. This year has pushed that awareness into those times I feel most fearful. Whether I sense Him as God of Peace or Commander, He is the God of the Future and I trust Him with mine. In His presence, fear melts away like the dew in the waking dawn.

Anyone can learn the drills. They teach them at Kaiser Wellness classes all the time. But those classes can't teach you the blessing of finishing the drill and finding the God of Peace right here with you in this place to help you with whatever freaked you out in the first place.

Aren't we incredibly blessed?

Nov. 27: Pilot…And Suffering with Jesus

Now I rejoice in what was suffered for you, and I fill up in my flesh what was still lacking in regard to Christ's afflictions, for the sake of His body, which is the church. Col. 1:24

SITUATION

As I prepared for the Bible study tonight, it suddenly dawned on me that the second orienting prayer (found on May 31) must include some statement about the suffering of Christ, as well as our perspective as believers if we encounter persecution for the sake of Christ.

When Jim and I planted churches, we took it as a matter of course that we would face various persecutions. We were glad to be "the point of the spear" of spreading the gospel into new territory. Since we dealt with it regularly, we kept a clearer mindset to bear it patiently for Christ's sake.

In the Sermon on the Mount, Jesus promised Beatitude blessings to people whose witness for Jesus leads others to treat them harshly. "Blessed are those who are **persecuted because of righteousness**, for theirs is the kingdom of heaven. Blessed are you when people insult you, persecute you and falsely say all kinds of evil against you because of Me. Rejoice and be glad, because great is your reward in heaven, for in the same way they persecuted the prophets before you" (Matthew 5:10-12).

We assumed we would periodically get to experience that Beatitude blessing and didn't worry about it. Frankly, serving in an established church for a while has made me flabby in this regard. I rarely suffer now and that mindset sort of fell off my radar.

Father, please forgive me for not remembering this whole topic more intentionally.

It completely shifts the internal process of coming to peace when we adopt Paul's attitude about suffering. And it affects more than just suffering for Jesus.

BIBLE VERSES ON THIS THEME

These other verses about persecution inform my thoughts today. I've highlighted the pertinent phrases:

"Therefore, since we have been justified through faith, we have peace with God through our Lord Jesus Christ…but we also **rejoice in our sufferings**, because we know that suffering produces perseverance; perseverance, character; and character, hope. And hope does not disappoint us, because God has poured out His love into our hearts…" (Romans 5:1, 3-5).

"I want to know Christ and the power of His resurrection and **the fellowship of sharing in His sufferings,** becoming like Him in His death, and so, somehow, to attain to the resurrection from the dead" (Phil. 3:10, 11).

"Consider it pure joy, my brothers, whenever you **face trials of many kinds**, because you know that the testing of your faith develops perseverance. Perseverance must finish its work so that you may be mature and complete, not lacking anything" (James 1:2-4).

NEW INSIGHTS

Wow! Pilot needs to orient big-time to this completely different worldview. This mindset views troubles as God's chosen tool to fashion me into a mature believer. It remembers that God highly values the perseverance that trials frequently produce.

This mindset views our occasional suffering for the sake of Jesus as a matter-of-fact reality and as a privilege and a blessing, not something to gripe about.

If all that's the case, it takes a ton of worry, fretting and fear off the table at one fell swoop.

It also shifts the way I would view the more trivial annoyances and irritations of regular life. When Pilot orients to remember these can all serve the purpose of bringing us to maturity, it's easier to embrace all kinds of trials with peace of mind. Everybody on earth suffers from time to time. Will I waste that pain or put it to good use?

O Father, May my reaction to suffering of whatever kind honor You and encourage others.

What a lovely goal!

Nov. 28: Grounding...And Finding Jesus in the Now

SITUATION

I've been focused on writing up my notes. Today I noticed with surprise that I had not practiced either drill this week. Since I didn't feel particularly revved up or shut down, I just picked Grounding because I hadn't done it in a while.

BODY CUES

Pretty calm and no worrisome body cues at all.

DRILL: Grounding

WHAT HAPPENED

I only got as far as FEET before I sensed the presence of Christ filling this room. I briefly wondered whether to continue the drill. But, hey, when the Lord shows up this way, it is an event. I sat quietly and paid attention. I got several blocks of thoughts all in a rush.

NEW INSIGHTS

The word "Goal" resonated in my mind. People do Grounding to reconnect to the here and now in this room. Back in January when He helped me refine my goals for the year, He kept them practical and anchored to a specific Bible verse. But, I see now that He has always had a higher purpose in mind.

- I don't do Grounding mainly to just collect myself when I've spun out.
- I don't do it mainly to return to Normal Mode.
- I don't do it mainly to reconnect Smart Brain, Emotional Brain and Body Brain.
- It's His desire that I do them mainly to fully reconnect to Jesus in the Now.

Nineteen years ago, He called me to a life lived in His presence. While I've found it pretty easy to do many things related to that calling, such as devoting my life to prayer and to helping other people connect with God, I have struggled to practice the presence of God on a moment-by-moment basis. I sense Him when I pray and I sense Him with me when nobody else is around. But I tend to go from one prayer time to another like a camel drinking deeply and then walking for miles to the next oasis.

I've struggled to develop that two-tier level of thinking, of continually staying aware and tuned to what's going on around me PLUS staying aware and tuned to the presence of Christ.

This year has helped me nurture that two-tier mindset in the context of the drills. I've been practicing all year an awareness of Pilot and an awareness of what Amy and Hippo might be up to.

All of a sudden I realized how easily I can apply that habit to practicing the Presence of Christ. It reminded me of that *Screwtape Letters* observation by C.S. Lewis that God wants His children to focus mainly on Eternity and on this present moment.

I love these moments when it's as if the Lord draws the curtain back to allow me to see the bigger picture. I have focused this year on mastering Survival Mode. These drills have been far more helpful than I expected. And now I see His bigger goal for my life and how this year has served mainly to develop more skills to live out my calling.

I see His goal for me, as someone called to a life lived in His presence. I'm a woman of peace who calmly practices the Presence of Christ. My body can find Him in the Now mainly by doing the drills. My spirit finds Him mainly through sanctified Pilot who stays connected to the Eternal Now.

14
Final Exam: Staying at Peace for the Holidays

Time to test what I've learned this year in a month that usually triggers me every which way but Sunday

Dec. 1: Pilot...And Trust Training Goals for December

SITUATION

For my entire adult life, December has been a difficult month for me to navigate. Most other Christians around me seem to easily embrace the holiday and the fun traditions and getting together with family and, most of all, easily worshiping Jesus as the reason for the season. People seem to love going to the malls for big shopping sprees to find just the perfect gift, which they seem to find with no trouble.

Not me.

During the other eleven months of the year, during my ordinary life, I deal with challenging aspects of my recovery at random times and seldom all at once. Mostly, I love my life the rest of the year. But all the fun parts of my life grind to a halt on December 1st, and it's like every trigger of mine, and every area of weakness or brokenness, steps up all at once and stays front and center all month.

All these challenges gang up on me at the same time.

- Greatly increased level of activity—way beyond my comfort zone of preferring to do only about two main activities a day.
- The pressure of having a Hallmark™ card kind of return to home, and cocoa-on-the-porch-enjoying-the-winter-snow kinds of moments, although thinking about my family of origin brings up mainly sad memories. And it wouldn't be wise to go home.
- The challenge to buy the perfect gift, an area I struggle with because I don't immediately know what to give. I'd rather crawl over broken glass than shop at the mall at the best of times!
- The mild but real anxiety of trying to coordinate the complicated schedules of ourselves and our two busy sons to gather for Christmas and birthday celebrations.
- I always struggle with my weight and it's a challenge every year to say No to the very things that tempt me most, front and center at one meeting after another.
- Perhaps the most difficult and ironic challenge is this. At the same time other people talk about Christ being the reason for the season; when they enjoy all the celebrations of the coming of the Christ Child, I struggle to stay as connected with God as during the rest of the year. Between all the extra activities and the little black cloud over my head that I have to be quiet about so I can serve others, I feel more alienated and anxious around God, not celebratory. That's one reason I look forward so eagerly to my January 1st prayer retreat. I miss feeling close to God during the minefield of December.

I've worked hard for the past ten years to whittle away at the triggers that turn this month into a source of dread. Believe it or not, it's been way better this year than it used to be. I spent two Christmas seasons really diving in to tackle the fears about money that used to paralyze me. I slew that dragon and started a Christmas fund which solved that part of it. *Thank You, Jesus.*

These days I have a much clearer sense of God's blessing over the strict boundary I had to set with my mom. The grief still hovers over this month like the Ghost of Christmas Past, but it's a more peaceable sadness. Yes, I had to build a wall, a quiet wall, but now it's covered with fragrant – and thornless – roses.

Just yesterday, our son Zach accepted a job offer to Idaho so that throws all our plans up in the air even more than usual. I'm thrilled for him and for April his wife. It's something they've wanted and worked hard to accomplish. However, it removes even the little bit of structure of previous Decembers.

I bring all of this before You and ask for wisdom. How can I handle these challenges this December? I really need a game plan. What would it look like to use what I've learned this year to help make this season peaceful and enjoyable? Most of all, how can I stay more connected to You this month?

You have given me Col. 3:15 as my assignment this year. "Let the Peace of Christ rule in your hearts since as members of one body you have been called to peace. And be thankful." This December, I ask You to show me how to find peace in this month that usually holds very little peace. And how can I stay connected to Your presence this month?

WHAT HAPPENED

As soon as I quieted my mind to listen, I was reminded of the story of the Angel Gabriel visiting Mary found in Luke 1:26-56. This story was the passage I sat in for a whole year, a few years ago. Jim plans to preach from it this Sunday for the first Sunday of Advent.

What do You want me to see today from this story?

I heard the word, **"Receptivity."** That year I realized that Mary was receptive to God's plan, and she responded by immediate yieldedness. I had spent that year cultivating Mary's quality of receptivity in my own walk with God. "I am the Lord's servant...May it be to me as you have said" (Luke 1:38).

As I sat quietly, I pondered this story in light of letting the peace of Christ rule. Gratitude welled up within me to my wonderful, multitasking Father when I noticed another of His ulterior goals. This entire year has prepared me and given me new tools to face this challenging month!

I felt a huge wave of encouragement that He would help me this month. I listened as ideas came to me about how to deal with these challenges. I've included the 3x5 card of my Trust Training plan of action. I plan to carry this card around with me and, with God's help, walk this out in December.

DEC 2018 GOAL: Stay at peace every day this month

- Be Mary: Focus on staying receptive to the God of Peace.
- *"Stay close to Me"* (at HQ, close to my Commander)
- Do one or the other drill (or part of the drill) every day this month and keep track of the days you do them
- Stay grounded to the Now (so do more of Grounding this month)

Dec. 2: The Peace of Christ…And Christmas Names

INSIGHT

The advent service touched my heart. The music moved me and I felt God ministering to my spirit through the songs and the sermon. Two Christmas names of Jesus jumped out at me in light of my prayer time yesterday.

Jesus is **Emmanuel**, a name that literally means "God with us." You have called me to a life lived in Your presence and You dwell in my heart by the power of God. This month I will seek You out as Emmanuel, knowing that You have promised to be with us and with me.

Thank You. Thank You.

The other name that leaped to my attention was **Prince of Peace**. I almost laughed out loud in the middle of the song set when I realized how long it took me this year to realize that the God of Peace is also the Commander of the hosts of Heaven. It took so long to realize how closely those two aspects of Your character lie side by side.

And then I find it here, spelled out big as life, linked together in one beloved title:

The Prince who rules. Gabriel told Mary, "He will be great and will be called the Son of the Most High. The Lord God will give Him the throne of His father David, and He shall reign over Jacob's descendants forever; His kingdom will never end" (Luke 1:32, 33).

The Prince who imparts peace. *Dear Jesus, I bless You as the God of Peace who gives us the Peace of Christ in all its blessing and fullness.*

I went home and added these two names to my 3x5 card.

Wouldn't it be cool to win back these Christmas names so elusive in past years?

Dec. 8: Grounding…And a Status Report

SITUATION

Well, it's been a week now. So far, the month has gone much easier than in past years. I can tell that working on the December issues for the past several years has paid dividends that accumulate each new December. I still feel that black cloud over my head of December ickiness, but feel encouraged that it gets smaller and smaller with each passing year.

So, here's a status report.

7 OBSERVATIONS

1. This month **I've needed to do Grounding much more often** because the main ickiness I fight is a sense of getting overwhelmed. I'm so grateful to have this tool in my toolbox this time around.
2. **Focusing on the Now** also helps a lot. I'm noticing that my dread of December fixates on the whole, unmanageable month. It's much less stressful to deal with one day at a time.
3. Zach and April's move has made it easier for me to **not sweat it about making plans**. There's no way any of us can lock down days. We all have to play it by ear and I'm good at doing flexible.
4. **The name Emmanuel** has become really precious to me this month. When I get quiet, I often sense Him as that name and He comforts me.
5. In fact, **all the Christmas stories have been especially rich with meaning**. Controlling my anxiety has freed my mind to embrace the sweetness of this month. The songs are more meaningful, and the stories more personal for me this year. After a whole year of focusing on the body, it's been especially meaningful to celebrate the moment when the God of the Universe took on a human body and a human nature to win our salvation.
6. On the other hand, **my body has been more vulnerable this month**. December still feels more like that day in the hospital where I couldn't come to total peace, but had to settle for actively compensating to balance out the higher level of intensity. The other night I had a pretty brief but intense conversation with Jim about something that troubled me. A few hours later, when I went to bed, I had the worst episode of heart pain I've had since March. It got so bad I had to take a Nitro pill, only my second this year. The next day, I felt weak as a kitten and had to rest for most of the day. That tells me I need to stay strictly at peace, no excuses, as my biggest assignment this month.
7. But lastly, **overflowing gratitude has made it a very good month so far**. After several months of focusing specifically on gratitude for all God has done to win our salvation, I notice that type of gratitude keeps me in an upbeat Pilot mode viewing my circumstances from a heavenly perspective, less tied to the ups and downs of a challenging time. Cool.

Dec. 12: The Peace of Christ...And the Ruling on the Field

Do not let anyone...disqualify you. Col. 2:18

Let the peace of Christ rule... Col. 3:15

INSIGHT

Last night our Bible study examined the part in Colossians 2 that includes the only other place in the New Testament that uses a variation on the word "Rule," found in my theme verse this year. My verse uses the Greek word *brabeuo*, and 2:18 uses the more intense form of that word: *katabrabeuo.*

What rich nuance this adds to my verse!

Brabeuo means "to arbitrate, to govern, to rule." It has the meaning of an umpire that makes a ruling on the field, like the ref at a football game or the line judge at a tennis match. My verse uses the broader word, *brabeuo*, where the ump or the king rules either **in favor or rules against**. Colossians 2:18 adds a *kata* at the front to specify that this umpire or king emphatically rules **against** the person.

At first, it worried me that I had gotten off the track to think in terms of the commander, not the ref. But when I went back to read that log entry, I recall so clearly how the Holy Spirit preached to my spirit that day. I relate more easily to the soldier analogy than to a sports analogy. I'm not much into sports. The soldier analogy gives a permissible rendering of this word. Plus, thinking in terms of the Commander and the soldier made it easier for me to identify "civilian affairs" and "earthly things," categories that made it simpler to figure out how to let the peace of Christ rule.

TWO APPLICATIONS

First, I feel encouraged to keep tweaking that second crafted prayer from May 31: "Helping Pilot Assess Earthly Things vs. Things Above." I had wondered if it was a stupid exercise. But if the analogy of these verses uses the sports visual, isn't that crafted prayer guide actually like the baseball rule book? Doesn't it make sense for us to keep track of previous rulings by the ref so He'll keep ruling in our favor, not rule against us?

Paul talked about it this way:

> Do you not know that in a race all the runners run, but only one gets the prize? Run in such a way as to get the prize. Everyone who competes in the games goes into strict training.... I Corinthians 9:24, 25a

This past year sure has felt like strict training with lots of time 'workin' it' at the gym. That crafted prayer helps me retain what I've learned this year.

It reminds me of when I learned how to do listening prayer and kept a running log of ways to test what we hear from Scripture and how to distinguish between God's voice and the voice of the accuser. (It's in the *Trust Training* book, by the way.) That running log became so internalized I no longer lug it around. It's second nature now to test what I hear.

So now, it's a great idea to keep a running log of clues on how to evaluate situations using the standard of God's peace. Hopefully, it will become second nature to find peace in all situations.

Second, it encourages me to realize that the God of Peace is a Player Coach who joins me here in the trenches as I "play the game" of my life story. Case by case, in one puzzling situation after another, He enjoys helping me figure out how to let His peace rule today. He's much kinder than an impersonal, critical or harsh ref.

Whether we mull over how to let go of anxiety and worries, how to deal with a messy relational issue or how to navigate through difficult days, He doesn't just give us thumbs up or thumbs down after the fact, judging whether we did it right or "Sorry, Charlie" if we fell short. As the perfect Pilot – calm, assessing, curious and kind – His calm presence actively helps us figure out what to do to face each situation. And then He walks with us through it, providing the very peace of mind He instructed us to cultivate.

Dec. 14: The Peace of Christ...And the Breaking of a Spell

Now may the Lord of peace Himself give you peace at all times and in every way….
II Thessalonians 3:16

SITUATION

It feels like my Decembers have been under a spell for years. Like Narnia, it's been "always winter but never Christmas." And this month I woke up. To my surprise, peace encircles it all. It's in the carols, on the advent display at church and in the message of the angels. After working so hard the past several years to tackle some aspect of December ickiness, I realize that I've been doing battle prep this entire year to hopefully break its power for good.

I hope so at least.

I had a sweet time with the Lord this evening and asked Him if there was anything He wanted me to notice. What is the nature of my December problem and how can I fix it? I sensed His loving approval of me for asking Him to teach me how to "do peace." I remember years ago realizing that I felt most comfortable in the dysfunctional feeling of constant angst and emotional turmoil that had been my reality for so many years. I had asked Him to teach me how to "do peace" because I had no clue.

He has been answering that prayer of mine. I know He has been at work because when people seek me out they leave with God's peace which has flowed through me to calm their hearts. He has taught me so much already but it has whetted my appetite to become a woman of peace always. I am not satisfied with bits and pieces, of moments of calm in the midst of stretches of fear or anxiety. I'm going for broke, asking Him to give me peace at all times (including December) and in every way per this Thessalonian prayer.

I saw that December has held the strongest concentration of leftover sadness and brokenness and angst from my childhood. My sense of ickiness stems from the very fact that this blessed month radiates and pulses with the peace so new and unfamiliar. I hesitate and dread December precisely because I'm still taking baby steps to learn peace.

Everywhere I turn, I run into the message of the angels.

Glory to God in the Highest and on earth
peace to men on whom His favor rests.
Luke 2:14

I sense His kindness and favor flowing over my life and all that pertains to me, His generous and lavish peace, expansive enough to bless anyone who comes near.

I hear His voice encouraging me to embrace the peace all around me.

So I embrace the peace I find when I step back into Pilot. I meditate on the peace of the advent candles and the peace presiding over Bethlehem. I enjoy the peace I've found with Jim and with our two sons in our extended Carpenter family. It took years of hard work to shift my emotional center of gravity away from my old dysfunctional family of origin to become fully present to the simple joys in this new family. Most of all, my heart overflows with gratitude for the peace I've found in the steady voice of my dearly loved Commander.

I hear His voice in my spirit:

> Arise, my darling, my beautiful one, come with Me.
> See, the winter is past; the rains are over and gone.
> Flowers appear on the earth; the season of singing
> has come….   Song of Songs 2:10-12a

Dec. 19: Grounding…And the Feet of a Deer

The Sovereign Lord is my strength. He makes my feet like the feet of a deer, He enables me to tread on the heights. Habakkuk 3:19

INSIGHT

The other day I had a precious ministry time with a good friend whose world has been rocked by one devastating sorrow after another. She hesitates to allow herself to begin grieving once again. So I support her, give her space to breathe, and help her brace herself while a torrent of grief washes over her head.

And I watch in real time as she experiences a hard-won and costly click in her spirit.

Her previous times of grief included an element of anger at God that she would eventually work her way through into acceptance and peace. But she has done such good work in previous cycles and this time around, I see her begin to understand and embrace the deep truth of tragedy that brings lasting equilibrium and transcendence.

Habakkuk 3:17, 18 captures it perfectly.

> Though the fig tree does not bud and there are no grapes on the vines,
> though the olive crop fails and the fields produce no food,
> though there are no sheep in the pen and no cattle in the stalls,
> YET I will rejoice in the Lord, I will be joyful in God my Savior.

The newbie Christian struggles to find peace when they face severe setbacks, disappointments and trying times. We're little rubber ducks at the mercy of the winds and waves of passing good times or hard times. And even in our good times we may not express gratitude with humble hearts because we secretly believe we're entitled to good fortune as our due.

But, in the life of every Christian beaten up by life, almost crushed by the troubles of this world, we watch for this evolution of response. At first it overwhelms us, and we know the grim comfort of Freeze Mode. The fear of having a panic attack makes us so vulnerable to panic and dread and we grieve the loss of any sense of safety. We despair of ever overcoming that awful residual weakness and vulnerability that shames us so.

If we do the work, if we doggedly pursue God even with all our frustration and anger and confusion, if we make our peace with Him time after time, we find the strength Habakkuk describes. God makes our feet like the feet of a deer. Not the gawky bird that struggles to remember we have muscles. Not the possum who checks out at the first sign of trouble. Not the Christian ashamed of her many fears.

We learn what my friend learns. It matters not the level of sorrow in this age. It doesn't touch our core for we are not citizens of this world but destined for another. Jesus has done us no wrong when tragedy strikes for He warned us ahead of time.

> I have told you these things, so that in Me you may have peace.
> In this world you will have trouble. But take heart!
> I have overcome the world. John 16:33

When our beleaguered little Pilot struggles to step back and assess in times of devastating sorrow, we grieve deeply but with indomitable hope in our hearts, not despair. **We can transcend all because we have expanded the circle of permissible sorrow to include absolutely anything that comes.** We trust that all of it is filtered through the all-powerful grid of our good God's permission. We have learned to face all that comes, but face it from our position of healthy, godly detachment that views it all as earthly stuff, civilian affairs. We rest in the knowing that it touches us only on this little blip of time we have left before we begin experiencing endless joy.

Thank You, Father, for using this year of experiments to help me connect that deep truth I already knew to my day-to-day practical habit of collecting myself.

These thoughts of mine center on Grounding this morning so I do the drill in light of Habakkuk's insight. I squish the floor with such gratitude for the blessings of this day.

Centered in my chair I spread my arms wide to rejoice in God my Savior. I thank God for the season when He taught me Habakkuk's truth and I learned the glorious freedom of "Yet." And when I stand and take focused steps around the room, I mentally shift from gawky bird to surefootedness.

I recall when He made my feet like the feet of a deer. It's why my soul can calmly brace itself while the torrents of my friend's grief wash over us without it troubling my own peace. I expand my vision of Pilot to embrace the exhilaration of treading on the heights.

15
One Year of Experiments: Results

How did we do on the three tests we set up for ourselves last January? And what conclusions might we draw about how to proceed from here?

Dec. 31: One Year of Experiments...And My Test Results

A RECAP

As you may recall, I have been in "scientist" mode this entire year, testing out a theory of mine and doing experiments about Flight, Fight and Freeze. By my estimate, I did the Stand-Down or Grounding drills a little over 220 days this year. This includes times I did it personally and times I did it with someone when I used the drills to help them learn how to collect themselves.

Even though I'm continuing to learn more while editing this manuscript to get it ready for publication, I've chosen to discuss only what happened during the 365 days of this test period.

So, without further ado, let's revisit the three measurable parameters we set up at the start of this experiment back on January 1. To refresh your memory, this was my theory.

My Theory

When we notice that our emotions and our physical body have slipped into Flight, Fight or Freeze Mode, if we ***first*** spend 2-3 minutes doing whichever drill best pulls us back into Normal Mode, and ***then*** pray, we will find it much easier to fully connect with Jesus and find the peace of Christ.

MY THREE TEST QUESTIONS

1st Test: The theory itself

When I was in distress, if I did the drills *first*, did that make it measurably easier to connect well with Jesus?

2nd Test: The Short Term Goal from the Window of Tolerance

Was I able to successfully and consistently pull myself out of Flight, Fight or Freeze using the drills, even when under extreme stress?

3rd Test: The Long Term Goal from the Window of Tolerance

Was I able to widen my Normal Mode range this year so I didn't flip into Survivor Mode as often? And if I did flip, was I better able to control the degree of my reaction to avoid the extremes?

TEST #1: THE THEORY ITSELF

Even though I had a hunch this theory was correct, it shocked me how amazingly well this strategy worked. In fact, you may recall, it worked so efficiently that, after a while, it sort of freaked me out…which led to my embarrassing little hiatus when I pulled back for a few months.

Looking back, I think **this strategy worked great for two reasons**.

First, it manages the fear that distorts our thinking. As Christians we know that we can and should cry out in our distress and that God will hear us and respond. But adrenaline truly does gum up the works and makes it harder for us to hear accurately. Fear compels Amy and Hippo, or Body Brain to take control. They do not process things maturely. And they certainly do not see the dangers from a God-centered point of view. The 2-3 minutes we spend collecting ourselves helps us reconnect to our more mature – and more thoroughly Christian – self.

Second, it efficiently calms down the rush of thoughts that only gets worse when we're stressed. As I noted in more detail on October 19, the drills help us to systematically collect *and quiet* Smart Brain, then Emotional Brain, then Body Brain. Those crucial few minutes of preparation make us much more receptive to God's presence. It allows us to actually do what Psalm 42:10 advises, to "be still and know that I am God."

Christians often struggle to hear the Lord's still, small voice because we can't seem to shut down the relentless Chatty Cathy in our head. Meditation experts teach many complicated and difficult techniques to shut her down. Who would have thought that a simple Stand-Down or Grounding drill would get the job done so well? No muss, No fuss.

TEST #2 THE SHORT TERM GOAL FROM THE WOT
Was I able to successfully and consistently pull myself out of Flight, Fight or Freeze using the drills, even when under extreme stress?

This was also an emphatic success.

As you may recall, Fig. 26, "Short Term Goal…," illustrates our state of mind at any given time. The middle area represents our mind when it's in Normal Mode, and not in Survivor Mode at all and we can live our normal life.

The upper area represents our mind flipping into Flight or Fight mode and **revving up** to literally (or figuratively) run or fight. The lower section represents our mind gripped by Freeze Mode that **shuts down** because it considers the threat overwhelming.

Fig. 26 SHORT TERM GOAL: RETURN TO OUR WOT QUICKLY

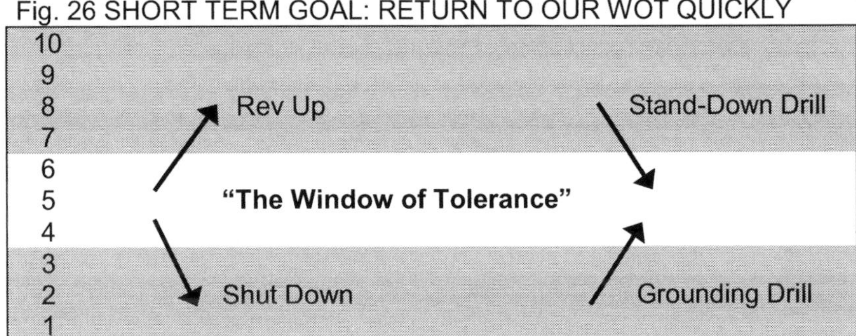

I would not have practiced doing these drills for such a long time if it hadn't been for this assignment. But I highly recommend practice, practice, practice because it's such a bone-deep reaction to flip into Survivor Mode and takes longer than you may think to really get it through our thick skull that we have the power to override Amy, Hippo and Body Brain.

Doing the drills on quiet, Normal Mode days taught me which body cues to look for and I became much more aware of when my body had begun to flip into fear, anxiety, anger or despair. That self-knowledge gave me a great sense of mastery and confidence that I had never felt before. Instead of passively getting sucked into a fearful state of mind, it felt great to know how to quickly nip things in the bud before Amy or Body Brain took over completely.

TEST #3: THE LONG TERM GOAL FROM THE WOT
Was I able to widen my normal range this year so I didn't flip into Survivor Mode as often? And if I did flip, was I better able to control the degree of my reaction to avoid the extremes?

Back at the workshop I used Fig. 27, "Long Term Goal…" to illustrate what happens when new recruits go to boot camp. By taking soldiers into "training mode" and deliberately putting raw recruits into dangerous situations, while teaching them what to do under fire, they lose much of their fear and can keep their wits about them when they're in actual danger.

Fig. 27 LONG TERM GOAL: WIDEN OUR WOT

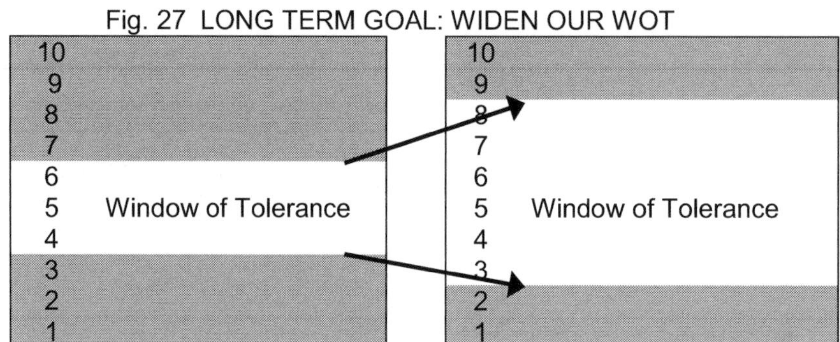

That same thing happened to me. I trained and trained on what to do in a crisis and when the actual crisis hit, especially when I had my heart episode, I stayed measurably calmer than I would have been otherwise – far better than previous times in the hospital. I even felt a bit like a trained soldier under fire that day in the hospital and felt almost euphoric when my training really worked.

In addition, I especially noticed my Normal Mode expand in a measurable way as the year went along. It expanded in four areas.

1. QUICK OVERRIDE. Since the drills helped me quickly reverse an adrenaline surge, that meant **I handled more situations while completely within Normal Mode** instead of partly from Survivor Mode. Before, if I happened to get hijacked, it took much longer for the adrenaline to drain off of its own accord.

2. ANGER. Also, especially as it relates to the hair-on-fire levels of anger of level 9 or 10, **God helped me to rid myself of anger and then put a fence around the upper end to say, "Don't allow yourself to get that mad again."** I logged the three main times I got really angry this year. So, this isn't a huge daily problem for me as a rule (all praise to God that He gave me grace to drain the abyss of anger I used to schlep around all the time!). But now, when I would get angry, it tended to get intense. I so appreciated God helping me to make sense of this and nail it down in a healthy way.

3. FEARS & WORRIES. I definitely saw measurable improvement regarding worries, anxieties and fears about the future. Doing the drills pulled me back into calm territory. But **God also helped me resolve a number of topics of fear. Getting that "click in my spirit" about the *What Ifs?* and locking down promises to stand on helped me quit shifting into fear mode about those topics.** And now, if I start to worry about something, it has become a well-established habit to remind myself of what I learned and immediately calm down.

4. SHUT DOWN MODE. Well into the year I noticed that I revved up much more often than I shut down. I realized that God had already used the *Trust Training* principles to greatly broaden my Normal Range when it comes to discouragement, emotional crashes and depressions. Weird as it may sound, I learned how to crash in a way that fostered resiliency.

So I don't crash as deeply anymore. And when I do crash, even if I get super bummed or overwhelmed, I have this bone-deep confidence that God will help me bounce back. I'm already a veteran soldier on that lower end of the diagram.

I noticed that trust training had already set a fence for me so I don't get clear down to the "#1" level any more. This year, I mainly struggled with Shut Down Mode for illness or low energy days. Learning to use Grounding helped me gain more of a sense of mastery for those day-to-day challenges as well.

What Next?

For God has not given us a spirit of fear,
but of power and of love and of a sound mind.
II Timothy 1:7(NKJV)

Congratulations to you, Gentle Reader, for finishing this book. I hope it has blessed and stretched you as much as it blessed me.

This year of experiments did me a world of good. Even though I've developed a new gratitude to God for giving us the gift of Survivor Mode – what an amazing and efficient system! – I'm even more grateful for this year that helped me to master it a bit more.

For so much of my life the limbic system kept me enslaved to my instinctual fears and my ego-driven insecurities. By facing fears and by training a Spirit-led Pilot to bring Amy and Hippo to peace, the stirring words of II Timothy 1:7 have become much more my lived reality instead of the wished for outcome someday out there.

After spending the entire past year settling one specific fear after another, I took my next prayer retreat on New Year's Day. The new theme He gave me circled back to the verse He used back on Oct 16 when I made the decision to go pro about my fears.

The new theme can be summed up in three words: **"Only One Fear."** We just finished working on settling this fear and that fear, this *What If?* and that one. God delights to deliver us from the fears of our earthbound story. But going forward, keep only one fear, one nourishing and blessed fear that will always enjoy God's wholehearted endorsement.

He recalls my attention to the gripping challenge found in Isaiah 8:11-13a, a passage that became my own this year.

> The Lord spoke to me with His strong hand upon me, warning me not to follow the way of this people. He said: "Do not call conspiracy everything that these people call conspiracy, do not fear what they fear, and do not dread it. The Lord Almighty is the One you are to regard as holy, He is the One you are to fear…"

These verses, one passage among so many that God used this year, now take center stage. What a lovely next step! I look forward to cultivating that reverence, awe and instant obedience as my heavenly Father continues to direct my steps and my studies.

Only one fear.

Cool. I can hardly wait.

So what about you?

Sure, I totally agree the drills are goofy. It's humbling to start at such a beginner level. But I encourage you to tackle your fears. I know it's scary but you'll survive. It will pay enormous dividends to learn how to master your own Survivor Mode.

Most of all, I urge you to get to know the God of Peace. He waits for you in those moments when the adrenaline surges and your heart sinks in fear. He has called you to peace. Wouldn't it be worth it to let Him help you to find peace instead of continuing to let fear run your life?

Let the God of Peace guide you into a deeper sense of His empowerment and your own agency. Let Him give you that deep assurance of His unshakable love for you so you become a channel of His peace to others. Let the Holy Spirit help you cultivate the fruit of self-control and break your bondage to earthbound fears. You'll love the freedom that comes when you rid yourself of the spirit of fear and embrace the joy of godly courage. Go for it!

Blessings on your head!

Appendix

The Prayer of Unpacking and Resting

The Prayer of Unpacking & Resting

Come unto Me, all you who are weary and burdened and I will give you rest. Take My yoke upon you and learn from Me for I am gentle and humble in heart and you will find rest for your souls. For My yoke is easy and My burden is light. Matthew 11:28-30

This prayer exercise is for people who feel weighted down by lots of responsibilities, worries and problems and who feel exhausted and overwhelmed by it all. Picture yourself like this hard-working soldier, weighed down by all the gear she must wear and keep handy to do her job. Even the protective shields weigh heavily on her back. Periodically she needs a safe place to offload it for a while.

For this exercise, picture Jesus here with you, this good soldier. You will be perfectly safe if you take things off for a while and rest.

This exercise has three parts: Unpacking, Resting, and Repacking. DON'T PEEK AHEAD. JUST DO EACH PART AND THEN MOVE ON. (It will take anywhere from 35 – 60 minutes.)

PART 1: UNPACKING

Come unto Me all you who are weary and burdened…. (10-15 minutes)

Mentally take stock of what you carry and take off items one at a time. Jesus is here with you, calm and gentle. He would be happy to hold anything you unpack and to keep it safe for you during this prayer time. Bring things to mind one by one. **Just NAME it enough to write down what it is but DO NOT engage to think about it.** After you write it in the box, mentally think of yourself as taking that one thing off your shoulders and setting it aside for Jesus to hold for these few minutes. Do this quickly, mentally focusing on **one** thing at a time, shedding each one in turn before turning to look for something else to mentally unpack.

Example: *My rebellious son*

Take stock. How are you doing? About this time I stretch my shoulders and roll my neck back and forth to check how loose they feel. I check in with my body for any wordless knot in my stomach or tension in some part of the body. Anything that's **"Not Peace"** is something to set aside. Now begin to **set aside your roles** in your world: at your job, in your family, as grown child, boss, employee, parent, etc. until you are simply "me."

PART 2: RESTING

…and I will give you rest…you will find rest for your soul. (20-30 minutes)

Now that it is just you – as you – here with Jesus who has invited you to rest, simply ask Him to give you rest. This is very gentle and quiet; probably not a lot of words, but more the sense of companionable quietness.

Invite Jesus to give you a verse to ponder in quietness or a healing visual image that speaks to your biggest need or one of His names that will refresh your soul.

As much as possible, if something intrudes that you unpacked in one of your boxes, just let the thought float on by. Jesus is holding it. You can take a break from thinking about it and simply rest. There will be an opportunity to pray about it later.

Focus on resting, on being. Enter into it. "Be still and know that I am God" (Psalm 46:10). (BTW, it's better to stay awake but if you happen to fall asleep that's understandable. Be at peace. That's ok. When you awaken, gently but firmly set your mind once again in the peaceful presence of Jesus and continue resting there with Him.)

You will sense when this restful encounter with Jesus comes to a conclusion or a finished place. At that point, jot down some notes about what happened. Feel free to pray about what you sensed and to listen to Jesus.

NOTES ABOUT MY TIME OF REST IN THE PRESENCE OF JESUS…

PART 3: REPACKING

Take My yoke upon you and learn from Me, for I am gentle and humble in heart, and you will find rest for your souls. For My yoke is easy and my burden is light. (10-15 minutes)

Now let's go back to that list of items we unpacked in Part 1. Let's not assume we have to put it all back on again. The whole point of Jesus' invitation in Matthew 11:28-30 is that He would be happy to carry much more of our load. So, as before, when we focused on one item at a time, do it again to each item on the list you compiled. Notice that you have empty space to the right side of each box. Use that space to close the loop about each item.

For each item, ask Jesus and check in with your now-more-rested deep self:

"Is this something I need to put back on since it's a responsibility or role I should carry?"

The answer may be "No"

It may be that it would be great to leave it with Jesus and let Him carry it. It felt great to totally off load it and you liked the peace of mind and lightness of spirit when He held it for you.

- It might be a **problem** that's beyond your control and only He is equipped to carry it.
- It might be a **person** you worry about, but you can't control their behavior and it might be best to let Jesus work in their life.
- It might be a **worry or fear** that weighs you down, but you realize that Jesus is here and you don't need to fear because He's got this.
- It might be a **big complex, mysterious situation** that He can handle much better than you.

For those items jot a note: "**NO. Jesus can carry this.**"
Pray a quick prayer to give it to Jesus and thank Him that He will carry it.
If you sensed a word of encouragement or a promise for this item while you rested, jot that down.

The answer may be "Yes."

The item might be an appropriate role or responsibility, a situation you can't get out of or an inescapable reality for you whether you like it or not.

For those items, jot a note. **"Yes."**
Then ask Jesus:

"What *advice* or *encouraging word* do you have for me that will make this load lighter or more manageable for me to handle?"

Jot down what you hear. Do this quickly but think about each box. Many items will be easy to sort out. If one or two are a struggle, then do the rest of them and come back to the harder ones at the end.

When you finish, take a final deep cleansing breath. Whew!
Say one last thank You to Jesus for giving you rest and a lighter load to carry.
Peace be with you!

Index of Topics

For further study or for more clarification
as you conduct your own experiments

Index of Topics

NOTE: Teaching items appear in Calibri font, log entries in regular Garamond

THE BRAIN

SURVIVOR MODE: Flight, Fight or Freeze Mode

FIGHT MODE…AND…

FLIGHT MODE…AND…

FREEZE MODE…AND…

GROUNDING…AND…

THE PEACE OF CHRIST…AND…

PILOT…AND…

STAND DOWN DRILL…AND…

ONE YEAR OF EXPERIMENTS

Made in the USA
Coppell, TX
07 September 2020

37125699R00160